# HOW TO BE A MODERN SAMURAI

## 10 Steps to Finding Your Power & Achieving Success

Antony Cummins

This book is a companion to *How to Be a Modern Samurai* (Watkins). While each can be read separately, together they form a connected work which aims to help readers benefit from samurai ways in modern times.

# ZEN AND THE SAMURAI SWORD

## Japanese Warrior Techniques for Agility, Clarity and Calm

Antony Cummins

## By the same author

### The "Book of" series

*The Book of Bushido: The Complete Guide to Real Samurai Chivalry (also available on Audible)*

*The Book of Ninja: The First Complete Translation of the Bansenshukai (also available on Audible)*

*The Book of Samurai: Fundamental Teachings (Book 1)*

*The Book of Samurai: Samurai Arms, Armour & the Tactics of Warfare (Book 2)*

### The "Ultimate" series

*The Ultimate Art of War: A Step-by-Step Illustrated Guide to Sun Tzu's Teachings (also available on Audible)*

*The Ultimate Guide to Yin Yang: An Illustrated Exploration of the Chinese Concept of Opposites*

*The Ultimate I Ching: An Illustrated Step-by-Step Guide to the Book of Changes*

### Books on samurai, ninja and Japan

*The Dark Side of Japan: Ancient Black Magic, Folklore, Ritual*

*How to Be a Modern Samurai: 10 Steps to Finding Your Power and Achieving Success (also available on Audible)*

*Iga and Koka Ninja Skills: The Secret Shinobi Scrolls of Chikamatsu Shigenori*

*In Search of the Ninja: The Historical Truth of Ninjutsu*

*The Lost Samurai School: Secrets of Mubyoshi Ryu*

*Modern Ninja Warfare: Ninja Tactics and Methods for the Modern Warrior*

*Ninja Skills: The Authentic Ninja Training Manual*

*Old Japan: Secrets from the Shores of the Samurai*

*Samurai and Ninja: The Real Story Behind the Japanese Warrior Myth that Shatters the Bushido Mystique*

*Samurai War Stories: Teachings and Tales of Samurai Warfare*

*Secrets of the Ninja: The Shinobi Teachings of Hattori Hanzo*

*The Secret Traditions of the Shinobi: Hattori Hanzo's Shinobi Hiden and Other Ninja Scrolls*

*True Path of the Ninja: The Definitive Translation of the Shoninki*

### Other books

*The Illustrated Guide to Viking Martial Arts*

*The Lost Warfare of India: An Illustrated Guide*

*For Jay Kane,*
*to help guide you along your own path*

**Zen and the Samurai Sword**

Antony Cummins

First published in the UK and USA in 2026 by
Watkins, an imprint of Watkins Media Limited
Unit 11, Shepperton House, 83–93 Shepperton Road,
London N1 3DF
enquiries@watkinspublishing.com

Managing Editor: Daniel Culver
Commissioning Editor: Sophie Blackman
Managing Designer: Karen Smith
Production: Uzma Taj
Commissioned artwork: Jayson Kane

A CIP record for this book is available from the British Library

ISBN: 978-1-78678-968-6 (Paperback)
ISBN: 978-1-78678-969-3 (eBook)

10 9 8 7 6 5 4 3 2 1

Typeset in JCS Publishing Ltd.
Printed and bound by CPI Group (UK) Ltd, Croydon, CR0 4YY

**The manufacturer's authorised representative in the EU for product safety is:**
eucomply OÜ - Pärnu mnt 139b-14, 11317 Tallinn, Estonia,
hello@eucompliancepartner.com, www.eucompliancepartner.com

A CIP record for this book is available from the British Library

www.watkinspublishing.com

FSC
www.fsc.org
MIX
Paper | Supporting
responsible forestry
FSC® C013604

# CONTENTS

# CONTENTS

# CONTENTS

# INTRODUCTION
# THE ZEN
# WARRIOR'S QUEST

*Zen has no secrets other than the serious contemplation of the cycle of birth and death.*

Takeda Shingen (1521–1573)

Are you struggling to discover the truth of Zen? Me too. Do not worry; the point of Zen is the struggle to gain the Great Realization, which means that if you are struggling you are doing something right. Have you been at it a long time? Again, do not worry; the Buddha's struggle spanned countless lifetimes and he had to start somewhere too.

So what is Zen? Answering this question is arguably more difficult than actually performing Zen itself. We will address the question in various ways, including by distinguishing between history and myth, and science and faith. Together we will set out on a Zen warrior quest and along the way I will arm you with the spiritual weapons you will need to engage in the fight to come, the only war there is, the conflict within your own mind. This is Zen.

Medieval Japan was a land of warriors, the *bushi* (武士), who are more popularly known as samurai (侍). These warriors lived by a strict code that was influenced by the teachings of Zen Buddhism. People may talk of cultural appropriation, but Buddhism was a positive form of cultural domination. How did this philosophy of self-refinement, which started in Nepal on the Indian subcontinent, journey over 3,000 miles and 1,000 years to find itself embedded in the military government of medieval Japan, and just how on earth did Buddhism, in the form of Zen, become associated with weaponry, particularly the Japanese sword? These are good questions and will be answered along the way.

Your journey will comprise five legs:

1. **Clean your mind**. In this section you will learn what is and what is not Zen, who the samurai really were and just what it is that we know about Japanese warriors and their relationship to the sword.
2. **Establish a form**. This section will help you understand how to structure your personal journey into swordsmanship and Zen and learn how the samurai did the same.
3. **Hone your mind**. This section will delve into the deeper parts of your mental journey, looking at key points to help you live your life without making the same mistakes over and over again.
4. **Engage the enemy**. This section will establish ways in which you can travel through life without conflict, while giving you the tools to deal with conflict should it arise.
5. **Become a Zen warrior**. This final stage will round up your journey in full and help you build a better picture of the path you can walk on after you have finished this book or even give you options to find another path.

These five steps contain 100 lessons to get you on your way to becoming a Zen warrior. This is the core of the book. However, there is also a sixth section featuring practical sword skills taken from ancient scrolls written by samurai masters. Finally, there is a summary list of bullet points to refer to and a glossary of key terms (see page 165).

Throughout the book, there are illustrations of the characters for some of the key Japanese terms we will encounter. You will see that the images have a sequence of strokes. These are to help you when writing out the characters for yourself by showing you the order and the direction in which to write the strokes. Calligraphy is revered as an important form of meditation in Japan (see lesson 22). The concentration required to render the characters correctly – particularly for a non-Japanese speaker – helps to drown out the mind's chatter.

By the end of this book, you will have a better understanding of Zen and be more familiar with the real samurai and you will start ahead of the game. You will be able to use your new-found understanding in various ways. Primarily, you will be able to face life and its harsh lessons with a clean mind, hold a truer understanding of the world around you and engage with the problems that you encounter.

Whether you are from a Japanese, Chinese or even Western tradition, you will be able to peek into the minds of warriors long gone to learn their secrets and flow with the same incredible dexterity and harmony that they did. For those of a sceptical persuasion, there will be ample science and rationality along the way to back up the spirituality and keep you from wandering into the realm of disbelief.

Before we start to navigate the world of Zen and the samurai, I am going to run through some key points. These address common misconceptions and so will help you to dismiss any myths you may have acquired previously.

## Zen Buddhism

- While the Buddha is considered to be a historical person, a sixth- or fifth-century BC Indian prince called Siddhartha Gautama, many of the stories about his life are legends created much later. Do not take everything you hear about the Buddha as fact.
- Zen is not Japanese; it is just the Japanese term for a meditation-based school of Buddhism heavily influenced by Daoism. Zen started in India and then developed in China centuries before it reached Japan.
- According to tradition, the first Zen master was the Buddha. Legend tells us that his line continued, but pinpointing where that line went is impossible.
- Zen was passed down directly from master to master. However, despite many schools of Zen claiming to have direct lineage, that link with the source has now been

broken. Modern Zen has evolved over many generations of dogma and interpretation.
- Zen is only one sub-branch of Buddhism, and historically it is a lesser-known teaching.

## The samurai

- Buddhism may not have originated in Japan but it has been there for 1,500 years, which is longer than the samurai themselves, who lasted for less than 1,000 years (from around the tenth century to the nineteenth century). The samurai were never without the teachings of the Buddha and Buddhism was a key foundation of their philosophy.
- Zen was an important aspect of samurai spiritual discipline, but so too were Shintoism, Daoism and Confucianism. Even Catholicism played its part, as some samurai were influenced by European missionaries who travelled to Japan in the sixteenth and seventeenth centuries.
- Before the sword became the primary weapon of the samurai, that distinction belonged first to the bow and then to the spear. Throughout much of the samurai era, most Japanese people were permitted to carry two swords. It was only in the time of peace toward the end of the samurai period that the carrying of two swords was restricted to the warrior class and became a famous emblem used to identify the samurai.
- Swords in Japan, as in other cultures, are a metaphor for "cutting through" delusions and so the sword has symbolic significance within Buddhism. This symbolism can help you gain more clarity in your life.
- Before the term samurai became widespread, *bushi* was used to refer to a fighting man. In this book I will tend to use the term *bushi* to avoid our progress being hampered by samurai stereotypes.

A final point: throughout this book I have included quotes from real samurai. Most of them date from the seventeenth century, but for ease they have been attributed to the modern book in which they are published. Those quotes that have not previously been published are just attributed to the original author.

# PART 1.
# CLEAN YOUR MIND

We are now about to begin the first leg of our Zen warrior's quest, the journey to clean the mind and clear away any misconceptions. Through the following lessons you will gain a basic understanding of Zen and the history of the *bushi*, avoiding the problems of language and pitfalls of translation. I will set you up with a starting point for practising Japanese calligraphy and engaging with the Japanese sword, and help you understand the human brain. We will investigate the cultural treasure of the samurai, and look at Zen's journey from India, through China, to Japan, as well as discovering how Zen is connected to violence. You will learn about the four great spiritual paths of the East, prepare yourself for *zazen* meditation and start to fathom the concept of karma and karmic debt, all on your way toward realization and enlightenment. I will help you understand the Japanese sword not only as a practical weapon but also as a holy artefact. But above all, you will learn to cultivate the mind of the beginner and you will realize that your starting point is to simply choose for yourself either the mediation cushion or the sword – or both. We will also investigate the importance of being fixed within your own time, and the importance of science and its connection to spirituality.

## Lesson 1. Become a Zen warrior
This book applies the principles of Zen to swordsmanship. By doing this, it follows in the tradition of the samurai, many of whom combined their spiritual and martial arts training, particularly in the later samurai period. However, as you set out on your Zen quest, know that there are many different paths

you can take. Zen will help you achieve mastery in whichever field you choose to pursue.

Assuming that you do decide to devote yourself to the martial arts, let us first look at some of the names given to practitioners of these ways. In Japanese, a *karateka* (空手家) is a person who studies karate and a *kendoka* (剣道家) is a person who studies the sport of *kendo*. However, this pattern of adding "*ka*" to the end of an activity to denote a practitioner of that activity does not hold true in every case. For example, you would not refer to a student of swordsmanship (*kenjutsu*) as a *kenjutsuka*. The title *kenshi* (剣士), scholar of the sword, is given to someone who has devoted many years to serious study, training and personal development in the way of the sword, while the even more prestigious title of *kensei* (剣聖), sword saint, is bestowed upon only the most accomplished of practitioners – and it is only ever used to refer to other people, not to oneself.

**In life you must follow a path or risk becoming lost in obscurity. The universe is waiting for you to start; you cannot wait for the universe to set you on your way, as the universe is infinitely more patient than you. It is time to make your move – no one else will do it for you.**

## Lesson 2. Look beyond cultural differences

As humans we are all driven by the same physical, mental and emotional needs and motivations. However, our fundamental alikeness can be disguised by cultural differences. For example, in the West, the age of enlightenment, which emerged in the seventeenth and eighteenth centuries, began to dislodge older ways of thinking. Logic and rationality took priority over unquestioning faith and superstition and slowly we entered the modern age. In the East this process occurred later and went in a different direction, but this does not make Eastern ideas on the self, the mind, existence and humanity any less valid.

Problems can arise when we try to force Eastern concepts to fit into a Western way of thinking. This misunderstanding can cause us to become lost in translation. Keep in mind that the way you think about things may not be the way others think. That being said, there is no reason that apparently perplexing Zen concepts cannot be absorbed into the Western mindset. We just have to loosen our ideas, which, when held too tightly, can act as tripwires lying across the no man's land of interpretation.

In the history of Zen, there have been numerous ideas that have been given fixed translations. Many of these are misleading today and are in need of updating. Throughout this book we will encounter these difficulties and try to find ways to overcome them.

**Linguistic and cultural barriers may stop you from understanding the true intentions of other people. When faced with a conflict, take time to consider if the disagreement is real or whether it is based on a misunderstanding. A lack of effort on both sides to really get to grips with what the other side is saying can cause small issues to get bigger. Listen first, act afterwards.**

## Lesson 3. Embrace the confusion

Now that you realize that your own perspective is something which you need to monitor, there is also the issue of the nuts and bolts of translation. Historical documents are almost always in another language or in an archaic form of our own dialect that is so far removed from the modern form as to be almost unrecognizable. The job of a translator is to convey the meaning of another writer, but this is not always done most effectively by direct, word-for-word translation. I just used the term "nuts and bolts". How could this be translated? A direct translation would not convey the meaning of this expression. This shows how treading the line between correct interpretation and direct translation can be a major problem for any research into the past – especially when it involves exploring another culture, as is the case with Zen.

Take the following quote by the twentieth-century Japanese Zen scholar D. T. Suzuki, in which he paraphrases the words of a Yagyu clan swordsman:

"Emptiness is one-mind-ness, one-mind-ness is no-mind-ness and it is no-mind-ness that achieves wonders … give up thinking as though not giving it up. Observe technique as though not observing it."

Suzuki has been criticized by some for presenting apparently incomprehensible statements like this one that can make readers feel as if they will never be able to grasp the essence of Zen. Such statements flood Zen books and Zen thinking, both old and new, and it can feel as though there is no wisdom to be gained from them. Until you can handle this style of presenting ideas through paradoxes, you will end up going down many wrong paths. Throughout this book I will help you spot statements like this and give you the tools to understand the key Zen concepts that they are meant to convey.

**Accept that Zen can be confusing. You are not the only one who feels this way. We all do.**

## Lesson 4. Choose your path

"Learn a martial art that you are especially fond of and remain within a single school until its deepest secrets have been discovered – this will also be helpful in the development of other skills."

*The Book of Samurai*

On this Zen warrior path, you are of course expected to study the way of the sword. However, first read this book all the way through before breaking off to do any of the exercises I have suggested. This applies not only to swordsmanship but to other areas such as meditation, calligraphy and the tea ceremony. Once you have read the whole book, you can decide to go down the path of the Zen swordsman or stick to the path of Zen only, or do neither and just use this book as a way to enrich your life. If you do decide to follow the way of the sword, then included within this book are a series of lessons on basic sword skills (see pages 137–50). These are taken from the original written teachings of the Yagyu Shinkage Ryu sword school and are fundamental to this school's style of swordsmanship. In addition to this you can follow my dedicated swordsmanship channel on YouTube called S.M.A.R.T. (Samurai Martial Arts Real Training), which can be found under the handle @SamuraiCombatives. Here I upload video instruction for you to follow and intend to do so for many years to come.

The Japanese term for swordsmanship is *kenjutsu* (剣術), consisting of *ken* (剣), meaning "sword", and *jutsu* (術), meaning "skill".

**You must pick a path, be it the way of the sword, tea, pottery, art, theatre, science or whatever. No matter what, pick a path and follow it with devotion. All people who take a path are searching for the same thing – meaning – but this can be found in any activity if you dedicate yourself to it.**

## Lesson 5. Know your brain and your mind

Zen trains the mind; sword skills train the mind and body. But it all starts with the brain. On average an adult human brain weighs about 1.3 kg (3 lb), is 85 per cent water, has the same electrical output as a small lightbulb and accounts for 2 per cent of overall bodyweight. However, beyond these basic statistics, there is much about the brain that is not fully understood and scientists have come up with various theories and models to explain its functioning.

One hypothesis, put forward in the 1960s by American neuroscientist Paul MacLean, proposes that the brain has developed three "layers" over the course of human evolution. The oldest, deepest layer is the reptilian brain, which governs basic survival functions such as breathing and heart rate and also instinctive behaviour. The next layer is the mammalian brain, which, broadly speaking, is associated with emotions. The highest, most recent layer is the primate brain, which is much more developed in humans than in other mammals. This part of the brain, MacLean argued, enables us to control our emotions and engage in complex cognitive, linguistic and physical tasks.

There is also the distinction between brain and mind to understand. Consider your brain to be hardware, while your mind is software that is powered by your brain.

By approaching an understanding of how the mind and brain work scientifically, you will be better prepared to address some of the older Indian, Chinese and Japanese concepts that have been absorbed into Zen. The most important thing to understand, though, is that we are subject to the same primal impulses and emotional drives, and have the potential to perform the same feats of mental reasoning and physical skill, as the *bushi* of the past.

**It is satisfying to ponder on the past, but this can become an indulgence. Take life lessons from our shared ancestors but do not become stuck in a fantasy. You were born here and now. This is the correct time, place and situation for you. Now your task is to figure out how to go forward correctly. The universe awaits you.**

## Lesson 6. Recognize your attributes

"If you are fighting someone who is physically more powerful than you, use swordsmanship when up close, and projectile weapons when at a distance. Above all, do not grapple with someone of such physical power; this is like fighting against water by using fire."

*The Book of Samurai*

Although we all have the same basic biological functioning, there are, of course, many physical differences between humans. Some people are measurably taller and stronger than others; some people are better adapted to the cold or the heat than others. Beyond these biological differences, there are also many variations in the way different people behave. Why does one person willingly charge a line of guns, while another flees? What inspires one person to detonate a bomb in a public place and another to give up their life to save others? At a less extreme level, why do some people wait patiently in line while others push in? What makes one person help someone who is in need while another will look the other way? Some of our actions are influenced by experiences in our own past, others may be cultural behaviours that have developed over many generations.

The history of the samurai is no different. The samurai were, in essence, indoctrinated child soldiers, trained to carry out acts of violence, destruction and brutality. However, a small proportion of them went beyond their conditioning to become masters of the mind and Zen. By following the lessons of these individuals we can hope to join their ranks. We can all overcome our cultural baggage and learn to simply be better people.

**We are born equal in worth but not identical in attributes. Always recognize your limits and play to your strengths, but also look to improve where you are lacking. We are not all the same, but that diversity is what makes our lives worth the challenge.**

## Lesson 7. Build your Zen practice on Buddhist foundations

"To go on a successful *shinobi* mission, you should take any measure to make your plan as flawless as possible, from the beginning to the end, before you take any action. Taking on the guise of a priest as an example, you should practise playing the flute very well and learn to talk on Zen."

*The Book of Ninja*

In modern times Zen has become fashionable, but in the process it has also become somewhat detached from its foundation in Buddhism. Before you can explore and practise Zen you have to know at least *something* about Buddhism. You do not need to become an expert, but you do need to investigate the essentials. Yes, you really do have to engage with Buddhism to practise Zen, I am afraid. Remember that Zen is just one of many offshoots of Buddhism. Does this mean you cannot meditate without being familiar with Buddhism? This is where it gets a little tricky. Of course you can meditate. Prayer and trance in other religions are forms of meditation and, yes, they are similar in nature to Zen meditation. The word Zen is just a Japanese rendering of the original Indian word for "meditation", but for your meditation to be truly Zen it must have a Buddhist foundation, just as Christian prayer is based on the tenets of Christianity. A small amount of effort will go a long way to making your meditation practice that much more effective, so it is best we explore Buddhism first.

**As a first step, take time out of each day to declutter your mind. Go for a walk, have a relaxing coffee, spend time in nature. Whatever you choose to do, the goal must always be to achieve tranquillity of mind. Sitting on a device or gossiping will not cut it. For at least 15 minutes a day, empty your mind and stop talking. After this you can start training yourself and building your life for the better.**

## Lesson 8. Find the truth

Now it has been established that you need Buddhism as a foundation of Zen, the question of what Buddhism really is arises. Protestants, Catholics, Methodists, Baptists – are they not all followers of Christ? They all follow Christ's teachings but they are not all the same. We have no recorded writings from

Christ himself, just as we have no record from the Buddha; all we have are historical accounts which claim to carry Christ's and the Buddha's true teachings. Your lifelong task is to find a truth that you can believe in.

Buddhism is divided into two main branches: Theravada ("School of the Elders") including other older associated schools; and Mahayana ("Great Vehicle"). Theravada is the supposedly older tradition and is widespread in Sri Lanka and Southeast Asia, whereas Mahayana predominates in East Asian countries such as China, Japan and Korea. Zen derives from the Mahayana branch.

Broadly speaking, Theravada focuses on the earliest Buddhist teachings, and Mahayana adds further layers of complexity. However, both systems share the core Buddhist teachings, which we will explore next.

**You will encounter people who will tell you that their way is the one true path, but it is for you to decide what is true and what is not.**

## Lesson 9. Understand the Dharma

"He studied Zen deeply and grasped its truth."
**Obituary of Hojo Tokimune**

Dharma is a term that is used in many of the main religions of India, including Hinduism, Jainism and Sikhism, to refer generally to the following of one's religious and moral duty. In Buddhism, it has a more specific meaning: it is the name for the Buddha's teachings. These teachings, which come from his realization of the true nature of reality, are central to the different branches and sub-branches of Buddhism.

The original term for Buddhism is actually Buddha-Dharma, which translates as "teachings concerning universal truths as told by the Enlightened One". However, without any written record from the Buddha himself, who lived in the sixth or fifth century BC, we only have parables and tales recorded by his followers. These sometimes date to hundreds of years after he was alive, and have been passed down over the many centuries since. There are also numerous Buddhist teachings that do not even claim to be from the Buddha, but are said to be realizations from masters who came after him.

However, do not worry about the complex web of Buddhist sources. Just focus on the following core teachings of the Buddha:

- *samsara*, the cycle of life, death and rebirth
- reincarnation
- the Four Noble Truths
- the Eightfold Path
- the Six Perfections
- compassion for other beings
- the Ten Ox-Herding Pictures
- *sangha*, the Buddhist community
- meditation, or Zen
- liberation, of self and others
- enlightenment
- *nirvana*, freedom from suffering and rebirth.

If you are going to become a Zen warrior, you need to have a foundation in Buddhism – and if you want a foundation in Buddhism, then it is best that we engage in a short exploration of these topics.

### Samsara

The circle of life, death and rebirth is called *samsara*. You are born, you acquire or redeem karmic debt through your actions during your life, you die and you are reborn inside of the universe. The goal for Buddhists is to exit this cycle because no matter who or what you are, you are bound to experience suffering, or *dukkha* in Buddhist terminology. "Suffering" is the most common English translation of *dukkha*; however, it can also be understood as "discontent" or "unease". Even first-world problems will trouble you if you pay them any heed. Suffering is inescapable while you are caught in this cycle. Zen is a path to enlightenment, which will enable you to exit the cycle of *samsara*.

## Reincarnation

You are alive now and you have been alive before. You have no recollection of previous lives and when you die and are reincarnated you will have no recollection of this current life. Often, we use the term "soul" to refer to the intangible essence that transfers from one life to the next, but Buddhists prefer terms like "conscious stream" or "mind stream". You may not be reborn as a human, you may not even be reborn on Earth; you could be a spirit, a demon, an animal, even reincarnated in another dimension. But your "conscious stream" is put into a new shape and you are subjected to the suffering of existence again, until you break the cycle and "dissolve" into *nirvana*.

## The Four Noble Truths

Also known as the Four Truths of the Noble One, the Four Noble Truths are statements on the reality of existence. They are:

1. Understand that you will encounter suffering in this and future lives.
2. Know that suffering is of your own making because you always want more than you have.
3. If you stop wanting more, suffering will become less.
4. To help release yourself from the cycle of suffering you should follow the Eightfold Path.

These four statements are at the heart of the Dharma. It is not enough just to read them; they can only be fully understood through direct personal experience.

## The Eightfold Path

This is a set of principles of behaviour based on the teachings of the Buddha. It is worth knowing these eight points and trying to adhere to them. They are:

1. Right view of the world (understanding the Four Noble Truths)
2. Right intention (avoiding hateful behaviour)
3. Right speech (avoiding saying things that are abusive or dishonest)
4. Right action (only doing things that do not harm others)
5. Right livelihood (avoiding doing a job that causes harm to others)
6. Right effort (putting effort into cultivating wholesome states of mind)
7. Right mindfulness (watching over your mind to guard against unwholesome states of mind)
8. Right focus (focusing your mind in a single direction – for example, through meditation).

If you apply these eight ways to your existence you will never go wrong.

## The Six Perfections

Running alongside the Eightfold Path is the concept of the Six Perfections, qualities that we need to develop in ourselves. These come from Mahayana Buddhism. There are more perfections listed in Theravada Buddhism, which has ten (including these six). However, as Zen is derived from Mahayana Buddhism, the Six Perfections are the most relevant qualities for us to focus on. They are:

1. Generosity (gladly giving others what they need with no expectation of reward)
2. Morality (virtuous, disciplined behaviour in accordance with the Eightfold Path)

3. Patience (tolerance and holding back in response to provocation; perseverance and endurance in the face of hardship)
4. Diligence (maintaining the energy and effort required to follow through on your intentions even when faced with obstacles)
5. Meditative concentration (perfecting your meditation practice to take you to a place beyond thought)
6. Wisdom (developing a transcendent knowledge that enables you to see perfectly the true nature of reality).

The Four Noble Truths tell you that something is wrong, the Eightfold Path explains how to move correctly though reality, and the Six Perfections help you hone your attitude.

## Compassion for other beings

While following a Buddhist path causes us to focus in on ourselves, part of this also involves showing compassion toward other life forms. You must help all people in need, be they friends or foes; in fact, you should avoid classifying people as friends or foes in the first place. Never kill that spider in the front room, never swat the fly, save the slug shrivelling on the hot pavement, be kind to strangers and avoid causing anyone a problem. Following these rules leads you toward the way of the Buddha.

## The Ten Ox-Herding Pictures

Coming from the Zen tradition, the Ten Ox-Herding Pictures (or Ten Bulls) are ten short texts each accompanied by a drawing. Together they represent the stages of a Zen practitioner's progress toward spiritual enlightenment. We will examine the Ten Ox-Herding Pictures in more detail in lesson 67.

## Sangha

The global community of Buddhists, who provide support to each other in their efforts to follow the Eightfold Path, is known as the *sangha*. An often-used analogy is that the Buddha is the doctor, the Dharma is the medicine and the *sangha* comprises the medical assistants. The quality of the support the *sangha* gives of course will depend on the people you interact with; this includes masters of the past who have left written records for you to follow. This community is what you lean on – but, remember, it is still *your* job to perfect your mind. No one else can do it for you.

## Meditation

This is the use of the mind to help you see the true reality of the universe. In short, the path you take to see the truth *is* meditation. There are two stages: firstly, calming the mind to reduce your thoughts and sharpen your focus; secondly, gaining insight into the nature of reality and releasing yourself from craving and thus in turn escaping from suffering and discontent.

## Liberation

True freedom comes in the moment that you realize you are bound by your own actions and you become so clear on the way forward that you never give in to emotion and cravings in this world. Instead, you are able to rise above base human desire and control your mind with perfection.

## Enlightenment

An enlightened being is one who has attained Buddhahood, who knows what lies beyond existence and has merged with the primordial truth. Enlightenment is the completion of all tasks, the relief from suffering, so that you live in perfect harmony with all people alongside the divine. After this, you will be ready to enter *nirvana*.

## Nirvana

After death an enlightened person moves on to the "other place"; that is to say, a place outside of known reality, from which that person will never again be drawn into the prison of existence. That place, or non-place, is known as *nirvana*.

*Nirvana* literally means "extinguishment". It is the absence of reality and the end of your path. However, be aware that the term *nirvana* is also sometimes used to refer to two preliminary situations that occur before the "ultimate" *nirvana* described above. These are:

1. a mental state in this life where you no longer feel suffering
2. a space where the pre-enlightened mind resides before full enlightenment.

Some Buddhists believe that *nirvana* is not another place, but simply represents the most perfect way to live your life. According to this version of *nirvana*, existence and reality never end, which would mean that the Buddha and all the other perfected beings are still here with us. It is your choice which you believe, because Buddhists argue among themselves on this point.

**In summary, Buddhists believe that we are all part of the cycle of birth, death and rebirth, that suffering and disappointment come from our own cravings and attachments, but that through right behaviour and meditation we can see the truth of our reality, liberate our "conscious stream" from this cycle and reach the ultimate destination of *nirvana*.**

## Lesson 10. Accept the known unknown

"When you give yourself up to Heaven's path and have an iron will and give no attention to your life, you will be free from thinking or reasoning and have no indecisiveness and achieve an empty mind."

*The Book of Ninja*

Often Buddhism will talk about "this shore" and the "other shore", as though you are on one island looking over a stretch of water toward another. "This shore" represents *samsara*, the cycle of life, death and rebirth, while the "other shore" is wherever you go – if anywhere – after you leave existence and reach, attain or enter *nirvana*. According to the dual-shore analogy, the teachings of Buddhism are like a raft on which to cross the water. For you, on your Zen warrior quest, Zen is a part of that raft, a vehicle to take you to the other shore and become enlightened.

Even the Buddha had to use terms like "space", "place", "over here" and "over there". This is because all humans are bound by the laws of physics and three-dimensional space and the limitations of language. There are no words in our shared vocabularies that can truly explain what is beyond reality, what is "outside" the universe. This concept has puzzled humankind for eons. Borders and edges are all we can see, no matter where we look: the garden fence, the sea shore, the horizon, the perimeters of sun and stars above us, they are all lines dividing one physical space from another.

It is true that dreams occupy another space; it is large and full of wonders and it is not defined by the physics of the universe. This realm of the imagination transcends the world of physical borders. Yet there is still a boundary between consciousness and unconsciousness, even if it can be somewhat fluid.

What it comes down to is that no one knows what *nirvana* is, whether it is the end of existence, whether we retain our consciousness there, or whether it is true oblivion. And even if anyone did know what *nirvana* was, they would not have the language to describe it to the rest of us. So when you read or hear descriptions of *nirvana* as another place, or the lack of another place, or a nowhere within nowhere, or a somewhere inside of outside, know that such descriptions are just speculations and have been limited by human language and thinking. The lesson here is that *nirvana* is a desirable state or destination, but no one knows any more than that.

**Do not get drawn into arguments about the nature and reality of the universe; the truth is that no one knows, and anyone telling you that they do know does not. There is either a great secret beyond the veil of life or there is nothing.**

**It is for you to decide what you believe, but it will only ever be belief not knowledge. Take Zen with you on your journey but never be bound by dogma. The key to awakening is to make your own discoveries.**

## Lesson 11. Grasp the lamp of Zen

Now that you have a grasp of Buddhism and its foundational beliefs, it is time to focus on Zen. After that, we will move on to the way of the sword.

Theoretically, Zen starts with the Buddha and ends with you. After much searching, the Buddha, without recourse to literature, secret chants or dark rituals, had the Great Realization and found what he was looking for. Subsequently, he attained bliss on Earth, and then, after his death, he left the cycle of *samsara* and entered *nirvana*. He had no worries, no trauma, no prejudice, no confusion, no hatred; he knew only purity and truth. He reached this state without drugs or intoxicants of any form. He saw the universe as it is seen by "God" and existence unfolded before him in absolute clarity. However, he was not the first. While various theories abound, there are said to have been at least seven great Buddhas who came before him, and, by rights, all of us should follow.

Legend says that one day, when the Buddha was preaching, he held up a flower to represent his new understanding, and in the crowd only one person understood his intention, just one of all his disciples who had access to his teachings. In turn, this person, whose name was Mahakasyapa, passed on the teachings, founding the line of Zen patriarchs. These are the select few people who have glimpsed the Buddha's truth throughout the ages. This tradition is known as the "lamp" and is the secret of Zen. The lamp represents the enlightenment that, according to legend, has been passed down to this day and is yours to find if you can.

**Some stories from the past definitely happened and some are legendary. While recorded history is important, sometimes it is best to take a leap into legend to bring out the best in yourself and others.**

# Lesson 12. Follow the journey from *dhyana* to Zen

"Pay proper reverence to the gods and study Zen."
**Takeda Shingen (1521–1573)**

What we know as Zen originated in India as *dhyana*; when it travelled to China it became *ch'an*; and when it reached the shores of Japan the word changed again, to *zen*. All three mean the same thing: "meditation" or "absorption". There is nothing mystical or esoteric about Zen; it is just the act of meditation and contemplation until one realizes the profound truth of the universe. Zen offers a great prize at the end of your quest: the experience of true happiness and understanding.

The fifth- or sixth-century sage Bodhidharma, the 28th patriarch of the Indian lineage, is said to have travelled from India to China, taking with him the teachings of Zen and founding the Chinese lineage of patriarchs. When Zen reached China, it became influenced by local Daoist concepts such as *yin-yang* theory, *chi* and the Dao. Daoism was about letting go of social structures and moving with nature, allowing a new state of mind to emerge, which complemented the principles of Buddhism. This was in opposition to Confucianism, another major philosophy prevalent in China at the time, which was associated with a tight control of society and of behaviour.

Soon afterwards, Zen spread from China to Japan, as well as Vietnam and Korea, and then, in the twentieth century, to the rest of the world.

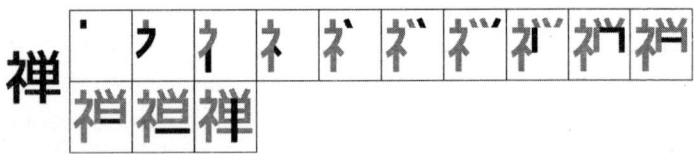

The Japanese character for Zen (禅) represents the foundation of meditation and your journey toward enlightenment.

**As it spread to different countries and continents, Buddhism evolved, absorbing aspects of the other faiths and philosophies with which it came into contact. In the same way, we should all be open to positive influences as we travel through life.**

## Lesson 13. Trace the growth of Zen in Japan

"Tendai Buddhism is for the imperial court, Shingon Buddhism is for the nobility, Zen Buddhism is for the warrior, while Pure Land Buddhism is for the lower classes."
**Proverb from the Kamakura era (1185–1333)**

Let us dig a little deeper into Zen history, as this will help you place Zen in its proper context before we start to look at its teachings in greater depth and integrate it with swordsmanship. Be warned: this can be dry, but it is worth it.

Zen was one of the first forms of Buddhism to arrive in Japan, during the sixth century, but it did not start to become prominent for another six centuries. Before the arrival of Buddhism, there was Shinto, an ancient Japanese religion that focuses on the *kami*, revered spirits which inhabit all forms of nature, from winds and rains to mountains and rivers. Just as Chinese Buddhism took on aspects of Daoism, so Japanese Buddhism absorbed some features of Shinto. Buddhism and Shinto continue to coexist in Japan to this day.

In the early years of Buddhism in Japan, powerful clans promoted the spread of this new religion. By the eighth century, it had been adopted by the imperial family; state temples were founded throughout the land and Buddhist monks were ranked in a hierarchy akin to that of government officials. Two sects in particular, Tendai and Shingon, jostled for prominence at the imperial court, whereas another sect, Jodo or Pure Land Buddhism, was paramount among the warrior and lower classes.

During this time Zen was a sub-branch of Tendai and was unable to establish itself as a school in its own right. However, that was to change in the late twelfth century thanks to a monk called Eisai (1141–1215), who journeyed to China to study at a Ch'an school for more than two decades. Returning to Japan as a master, he resolved to build up the influence of Zen. As we have seen, Buddhism at this time was extremely political and Master Eisai could not contend with the established factions in the imperial capital of Kyoto. His "new" idea of Zen was not well received, and so he looked elsewhere for an opening. Travelling to the military capital of Kamakura in the east, he found favour with the first shogun, Minamoto no Yoritomo. Following Yoritomo's death in 1199, the shogun's widow and regent, Hojo Masako, continued to support Eisai.

Master Eisai was no ragged monk on a spiritual quest. He knew that Zen would take time to establish and so had not given up his older Buddhist ways. This allowed him to maintain influence, power and wealth while planting the "seed of Zen" among the samurai elite. While Eisai started Zen on a journey toward its final partnership with the Japanese sword, there was still much work to be done.

Another major figure in Kamakura to promote Zen was Hojo Tokiyori (1227–1263), a powerful samurai who became regent to the shogun in 1246. Under Tokiyori, the samurai embraced the meditative nature of Zen as they had never done before. However, at this point, the ways of Zen and the Japanese sword were yet to merge. The samurai weapon of choice was the bow and the idea of Zen within martial arts teaching was not common at this time. The samurai kept their military and religious lives largely separate and these two important aspects of the warrior outlook did not become fully synergized until the seventeenth century with the emergence of what I term *dojo* culture.

The flourishing of Zen changed the face of Japan. Previously, the country had taken its visual aesthetic from Chinese culture, especially the Tang Dynasty, which favoured brightness and colour in everything from architecture to the tea ceremony.

However, with the rise of Zen came the decline of flamboyancy and the adoption of a more austere ideal in all walks of life. The samurai became very serious. Stoicism became a focus in military strategy and martial arts and there was a genuine attempt to access the wisdom of the Buddha through Zen meditation.

**Be careful not to lose the thread of the Buddha's teachings in the complexities of history, political power plays and military strategy.**

## Lesson 14. Know the different schools of Zen

As Buddhism travelled throughout India, China, Japan and, of course, throughout history, it began to be codified, structured and formatted into different schools, leading to variations on the idea of the one truth, a true oxymoron. The pattern of religious division and subdivision can be traced back as far even as the time of the Buddha, which is when China was entering its Hundred Schools of Thought period. This was an era when various influential philosophies were vying for cultural domination.

The Zen branch of Buddhism was itself subdivided into five major schools, which are listed here by their more common Japanese names:

1. Igyo school – which specialized in symbols
2. Rinzai school – which specialized in paradoxical riddles called koans
3. Soto school – which specialized in seated meditation
4. Ummon school – which also specialized in koans but died out in the early twelfth century
5. Hogen school – which dwindled in the tenth century.

This brings us to the end of a basic history of Zen and its Buddhist roots. If digested correctly, this will allow you to enter into Zen with a more informed outlook.

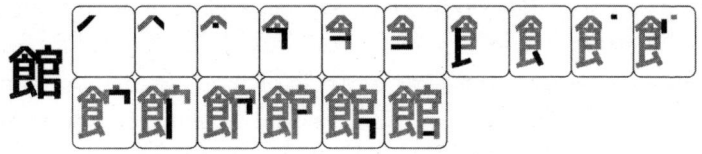

Some Zen schools and martial arts dojos are referred to by the Japanese character *kan* (館), meaning "house". Whereas, martial arts schools in general are referred to by a different character: *ryu* (流), meaning "flow".

**For you on your journey it may be best to boil things down to basics and avoid focusing on the differences between the various schools of Zen. Stick to practical meditation, clearing the mind and honing your reactions and reflexes. Never forget what your journey is about: self-improvement, both mental and physical.**

## Lesson 15. Embark on the way of the sword

"What makes swordsmanship come closer to Zen than any other art that has developed in Japan is that it involves the problem of death in the immediately threatening manner."

D. T. Suzuki (1870–1966)

Let us now start our journey into understanding the sword. What most people do not realize is that we just do not know how a samurai used his sword until the seventeenth century. Before then, all we have are general references to combat in the literary classics, and various combat skills are referred to by name but not covered in any more detail than that. In the late sixteenth century, Jesuit travellers to Japan remark on the effectiveness of the *bushi*, but do not describe their actual skills. The first detailed descriptions of how the Japanese fought appear in Chinese and Korean accounts dating from around 1600. Soon after this we get *The Book of Family Traditions on the Art of War* by Yagyu Munenori and the famous *Book of*

*Five Rings* by Miyamoto Musashi (more correctly translated as *The Book of Universal [Fighting Skills]*), which gives great detail on the samurai fighting style. There is then a flurry of treatises on combat, with an annotated picture scroll from the Yagyu family being the most famous in the world of Japanese sword craft. These skills have been reconstructed in the online documentary *This Is Kenjutsu*, which, at the time of writing, is available on YouTube.

The Japanese term *ko-ryu*, meaning "old school", is often used to refer to the martial arts of the samurai era. (It can also apply to other traditional Japanese arts, such as flower arranging and calligraphy.) While some sword schools claim to date from the fourteenth and fifteenth centuries, their age may be somewhat exaggerated. Besides which, there are no records of the actual techniques used in these early times and it is fairly certain that the sword skills these schools teach today bear almost no resemblance to the originals beyond the name of the skill. This does not mean that such schools did not exist in samurai times or that the samurai were not taught how to fight. We know that they were, but we cannot just bypass centuries of change to reveal the original medieval samurai way of the sword in all its practicality.

To add further layers of confusion, the Japanese arts of war were said to have been passed on by ancient gods from before the time of the samurai. According to tradition, heavenly spirits known as *tengu* would teach the deepest secrets of swordsmanship to chosen warriors. Even more mysteriously, a deity was said to appear in a dream or a vision to reveal skills to a sword master.

Such stories mostly arose during the Edo period (1603–1867), a time of prolonged peace when samurai sons needed to find ways other than waging war in order to earn a living. This was the reason for the rise of *dojo* culture. The move away from the battlefield to the training hall signalled a transition in swordsmanship, which moved away from the practical to the symbolic. The new style was described as *kaho* or "flowery".

Bamboo swords were invented to minimize the risk of injury, pads were worn for protection, duels to the death were made illegal and bouts of sparring between the various schools grew in popularity, all of which led to the growth of recreational sports like *kendo*.

Just because swordsmanship was no longer a matter of life and death, we cannot conclude that *bushi* from the period of peace were less skilled than their forebears. What we can be fairly sure of is that they had more time to explore Zen and connect it to practices they loved, not only the way of the sword but also, for example, the ways of tea and of calligraphy.

**Zen swordsmanship is a product of its time. Samurai during the period of peace put their efforts into both Zen and swordsmanship, and this should be your goal too. No longer an instrument of death, the sword becomes a symbol of your will to achieve. But you must take that symbolism seriously: train hard and do not just fantasize.**

## Lesson 16. Be aware of the sword as a holy item

"A poem states that if you have a sword in your spirit to cut off any doubts, dreams will be realized."

*The Book of Ninja*

Swords in Buddhism are not meant to harm other humans, they are used for the cutting away of negative aspects. Some Buddhist deities carry a sword to cut through greed, anger and stupidity. One example is Fudo Myo-o, who carries a sword to destroy the enemies of Buddhism. Another example can be found in the treatise *The Sword of Taia* by the monk Takuan. The sword named in the title is a legendary weapon that symbolizes inner clarity.

The concepts of the "life-giving sword" and the "death-dealing sword" and the "sword of no-sword" are prominent in Japanese martial arts, which are awash with Zen philosophy. These will all be covered in greater detail in later lessons.

Japanese culture attaches a particular reverence to the sword. One of the three royal treasures of Japan is a sword; swords are worshipped at Shinto shrines across the country; and, of course, the sword has been especially important to the *bushi* since the great sixteenth-century leader Toyotomi Hideyoshi banned peasants from owning and wearing them. Swords have been worshipped in Japan since ancient times, but this does not mean that *all* swords were holy. Although today samurai swords are highly prized by collectors as works of art, in the age of the samurai most swords would have been seen as nothing more than the tool of a warrior's trade. Only particularly finely wrought examples would have been valued as anything beyond that.

More often than not, the *bushi's* main focus of worship was not their sword but Hachiman, the god of archery and warriors. Larger samurai houses would have battle armour dedicated to Hachiman placed on a dais as a spiritual focus.

**The Zen sword is as much a symbol as a practical item. Use it as a weapon in your mind to cut away negative thoughts and emotions. In this way, you can become a master of Zen sword craft without ever touching a physical sword if you do not want to.**

## Lesson 17. Be aware of the sword as a status symbol

People often say that only the samurai were permitted to wear two swords, usually a long one (*katana*) and a short one (*wakizashi*), a combination that was known as the *daisho*, and that for everyone else the wearing of swords was banned. This is largely true. Before the disarming of the peasants in the late sixteenth century many people wore two swords, and after the change in the law there is evidence of famers complaining about their loss of rights. However, swords were not actually fully banned, neither were guns, they were just heavily regulated. Non-samurai could still own a sword, but their right to take it out of the home was severely restricted.

Swords have always been a symbol of power because they could be used in combat to gain power, but it was only after the sixteenth century that the "samurai sword" became a symbol of the entire samurai class. Around the year 1600 the concept of Zen and the sword as a samurai pathway became more established because the samurai were now associated with the sword more than any other weapon. Before this, the focus was on military strategy and the actual winning of wars and Zen was a separate subject of study. When the sword became the symbolic focus of the samurai, it merged with Zen to generate two-and-a-half centuries of training material for Zen warriors in preparation. This is the system that we will draw upon in the rest of the teachings.

**In life, practicality must take precedent. High-minded theory is all well and good, but if your theories are not getting you anywhere, then know that it is time to switch to a more direct approach.**

## Lesson 18. Enter the *dojo*

Traditionally martial arts are performed in a *dojo* (道場) but most schools of Zen practise in a *zendo* (禅堂). *Dojo* means the "place of the Way", while *zendo* means "hall of Zen"; both imply a place of training, progression and refinement. The origins of this kind of institution can be traced back to India, where special buildings were used to train students. While they do have a long history, you do not need to attend a *dojo* or a *zendo* to help you on your way. The Buddha did not have one, nor did many of the most famous *bushi*, who typically trained outdoors.

The *dojo* itself has various spiritual requirements; for example, it should have a Shinto altar and it should be clean. In Japan, *dojos* tend to be like Zen halls – clean, spartan and simple – but this is not true in every case. Many traditional *dojos* are filled with weapons, items of memorabilia, pictures and so on. Following the global spread of Zen and Japanese martial arts, *dojos* and *zendos* can be found all over the world. Choose one that feels right for you or choose to do things your own way, if you prefer

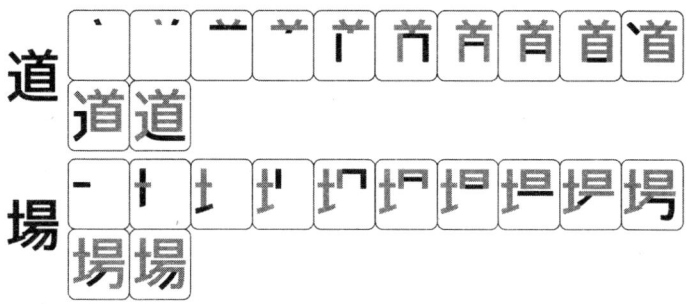

*Dojo* (道場), a place where martial arts are practised, is made up of the Daoist term *do*, meaning "the Way", and *jo*, meaning "place". The term *do* is often found in the names of martial arts, such as *judo*, *kendo* and *karatedo*.

**It would be great if everyone had a dedicated spiritual place to do their training. But remember that the thing that makes places like churches, mosques, temples or *dojo*s special is the community of people that gather there. Before there were Buddhist temples, the Buddha used to teach in the streets with his followers. You too can train anywhere you like.**

## Lesson 19. Know the history of Zen and violence

"Originally, military tactics, swordsmanship or any kind of art to kill others were about defeating an unprincipled but powerful man."

*The Book of Ninja*

Zen is a religion of peace … except when it is not, which has been for much of its history. The samurai used Zen to improve their ability to carry out violent acts even if they pretended otherwise. The *sohei* (僧兵) warrior monks were not dissimilar to the samurai. They wore armour and trained in martial arts while still following the ways of the Buddha. The distinction between *sohei* and samurai is that the samurai fought for lord and lands, while the *sohei* fought to protect their monastic order.

Early on in Japanese history, temples and monasteries had standing armies of their own filled with holy warriors ready to fight for political causes. The Ikko-ikki, which was the militant arm of the Pure Land Buddhist sect, fought a long campaign against the powerful samurai leader Oda Nobunaga in the 1570s. Although Nobunaga eventually triumphed, the Ikko-ikki were tenacious foes.

While a samurai was a samurai and a monk was a monk, the line between the two was more blurred than many people realize today. This is partly because they both practised Zen and partly because samurai often became monks. The monk known as Suden (1569–1633) started out as a samurai, fighting under his father and killing three prestigious enemies in battle. Having changed paths, he rose to become the leader of two major Buddhist monasteries in the heart of Kyoto. He also had a political career, travelling to the city of Edo and entering service as the shogun's secretary of state.

When a temple was built for Suden, it adopted an insignia of three black stars on its banner, which represented the three heads he had taken in battle – indicating that he was still celebrated as much for his military prowess as for his religious achievements.

**When it comes to the relationship between Zen and violence, do not follow the example of the samurai and the warrior monks. Non-violence should be your ultimate goal. Never use a spiritual path to promote violence, and, if you lapse into violence, never use spirituality or religion to justify your behaviour.**

## Lesson 20. Take time to meditate

Having looked briefly at Zen, its teachings, history and connection to the samurai, it is time to ask questions about meditation itself. Remember, the word Zen is the Japanese rendering of the Chinese and Indian words for "absorption" or "meditation" and refers to the state in which the Buddha sat when he became enlightened. Controlling the mind and seeing universal truths are the primary goals of meditation.

Meditation can be divided into three basic aspects:

1. Focused meditation. This involves stilling the mind by concentrating on something like an image or your own breathing until your mind becomes calm.
2. Open monitoring. This is about being aware of, or monitoring, thoughts that come into your mind. You should not be worried if this happens. Just allow thoughts to appear and then dismiss them until your mind becomes quiet.
3. Contemplating reality and truth. Once your mind is quiet and calm, you are seeking to perceive the world around you without distortion, to analyse the workings of your mind, and finally to see the truth of the universe (no small feat). This is the path to realization. There are many ways found in different religions worldwide that help us to get there. It is your job to become enlightened; you cannot just wait for it to happen. Even Zen's path to spontaneous enlightenment is not very spontaneous, as it can take a lifetime, or many lifetimes, of work.

Meditation, the simplest of things to do, has become one of the most over-intellectualized subjects in the world. Zen's whole position is that you should just sit and clear your mind until you gain a realization. That is all there is to it. For some, the practice of *nembutsu* is enough. *Nembutsu* involves repeatedly chanting a veneration of the Buddha – "Namu Amida Butsu" (meaning "Hail to Amitabha Buddha"). There is nothing intellectual about it, nothing complex, it is just a constant rhythm. Meditation, like worship, has myriad approaches and variations, but its aim is always fundamentally the same – to achieve clarity of mind.

The Buddha's approach to meditation travelled from India through China, where it picked up a lot of Daoist influence, before it reached Japan. There, Zen was often taught by Chinese monks. Small differences in method began to emerge between schools. For example, members of the Rinzai school would face inward in their Zen halls, while those of the Soto school would face outward. Similarly, in Christianity, the Catholic cross usually depicts the crucified Jesus, whereas the Protestant cross tends to be empty. Such distinctions may appear trivial but can become a serious issue to members of the different schools or denominations. For the true path-seeker, these details have no power and should never cause concern.

**Take time to still your mind, let crazy thoughts come in and fade away. After you have quietened your mind's chatter, start to philosophize about the world, about the nature of reality, about the spiritual laws guiding us all and about the great secret behind the veil of life.**

## Lesson 21. Practise *zazen* and other forms of meditation

The main kind of meditation you will come across in Zen is *zazen* (座禅). This is a Japanese rendering of the Chinese term *zuochan*, meaning "seated meditation". However, you do not have to be sitting to meditate; there are other ways, such as walking, or forming sand patterns, or following intense breathing patterns, or making what seem like erratic movements. *Chado* (茶道), the tea ceremony, is another way to meditate, as is *shodo* (書道), calligraphy, or *kyudo* (弓道), archery, and let us not forget *iaido* (居合道), the art of drawing a sword from its scabbard. Interestingly, *kendo* (剣道), which translates as "the way of the sword", is not generally seen as a form of meditation but instead has evolved into a sport.

It could be said that *zazen*, the way of seated meditation, is the highest form, because it is the way that the Buddha is believed to have meditated and because it involves no focus other than meditation itself. We actually have no idea what method the Buddha used under his *bodhi* tree. People have pondered this point for centuries. However, *zazen* appears to be the most likely. So, find a cushion and get ready for daily practice.

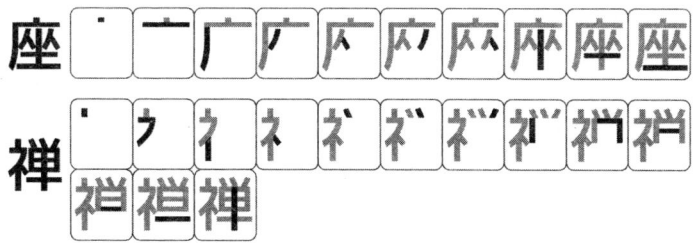

The characters for *zazen* (座禅) mean "seated meditation". The way we have shown is the newer version; the older way is: 坐禅.

**Find opportunities for meditation in your everyday activities. Sweeping the floor, washing the pots, mowing the lawn, any of these chores will do. But remember that your focus is controlling your thoughts, clearing your mind and contemplating the reality of nature and your own attachments to the physical world. Do not mistake daydreaming for beneficial meditation.**

## Lesson 22. Practise Japanese writing

Like much else in Japanese culture, the characters used in Japanese writing were imported from China. They are known as *kanji* (漢字), which simply means "letters". In Japan the practice of calligraphy is treated as a form of Zen meditation known as *shodo* (書道), and is undertaken with the utmost seriousness. There are many competitions at regional and national level, and awards are given to the most skilled calligraphers.

As we move along on our journey I will give you certain Japanese words to write out, including the one below (and ones in some of the previous lessons of this chapter). All you will need is a pen and paper, or you could use a brush and ink. Each *kanji* image contained within this book will have a sequence of strokes to show you the order and direction. If you want to deepen your practice of this form of meditation then I would recommend that you also read the book *Shodo: The Practice of*

*Mindfulness Through the Ancient Art of Japanese Calligraphy* by Rie Takeda (Watkins, 2022).

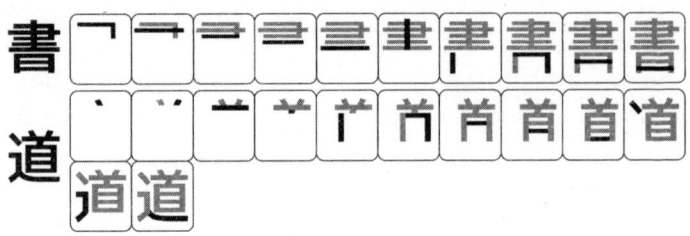

The Japanese term *shodo* (書道) is constructed using the word for "writing" and the word for the Daoist "Way".

**When we write something down, which is less often than it used to be, we tend to scrawl to get the job over and done with as quickly as possible. Along this path, take your time over writing by hand – whether it be a letter, a shopping list, or even just writing for the sake of writing. The written word is a great gift passed down to us by our ancestors. Cherish it.**

## Lesson 23. Learn how to meditate

The first major step toward finding perfect calm here and now is learning the art of meditation. The primary aim of meditation is to quieten the mind and the internal dialogue within, in order to take you to a place where you "float" in a new state of consciousness. None of this is magical, you just have to put some effort in. From this position, focus harder, working toward spontaneous realization and contemplation of the nature of reality from an uncluttered angle. Do not fall for the false idea that you just "wait around" in Zen; although meditation is typically done in a sitting position, it is not just sitting about. Your mission is to focus on internal clarity and provide yourself with a healthy mind-state.

Next, we will look at how to prepare for meditation and explore some basic meditation methods.

## Set-up

1. Set a timer. If you are new to meditation, start at two minutes and then gradually increase the time to ten minutes as you become more experienced.
2. Sit on a cushion and cross your legs. You will be spending a lot of time sitting on this cushion, so finding one that is a comfortable size and shape for your height, weight and level of flexibility will really help (see also lesson 34).
3. Relax your hands in front of you and keep your back as straight as you can. Breathe slowly.

## Method 1: Count to ten

Count your breaths slowly, start at one and try to get to ten. Each time you lose focus and an intrusive thought appears, start again from one. I promise, you will rarely ever complete this task. Stop when the timer goes off, even if you have not got to ten.

## Method 2: Calm the waves

Imagine the moon over a stormy sea. Focus on the waves calming as the storm abates until the moon is clearly reflected in the gently lapping water. Stop when the timer goes off, even if the storm is still raging.

## Method 3: Contemplate a holy image

Focus on a religious symbol that has meaning to you – for example, an image of the Buddha or a Buddhist saint, or perhaps a Sanskrit character. Every time a thought pops into your head, calmly acknowledge the thought and then return your focus to the image. This way is sometimes supported by chanting a mantra. Stop when the timer goes off.

## Method 4: Exhaust all thoughts

Allow any thought to come into your head. Do not latch on to it or play it through; instead, just observe it until it dissolves. Let the next thought in and quietly allow that to pass too. Be careful not to engage with your thoughts or you will end up daydreaming. Do this until the thoughts become less frequent or even, if possible, until they stop arriving at all. Stop when the timer goes off even if the thoughts are still coming.

## Method 5: Practise the swordsman's way

Imagine a piece of blank paper or a white screen in front of you. Every time a thought comes on to that paper or screen in the form of words or a picture, cut it down with your internal *katana*. Let the paper or screen break in two, revealing a new blank one behind it. Do this for any thought emerging until the white space in your mind remains constantly blank. Stop when the timer goes off, even if you are still having to wield your sword.

**Find your preferred way to stop the constant mind-chatter. Like eating, thinking is an essential part of being alive, but uncontrolled thoughts can weigh your mind down with stress and delusion. This is the start of your Zen journey – make your first step bold and purposeful.**

# Lesson 24. Understand karma

"Get close to monks and ask them about karma from the path of Buddhism; however, you do not have to enter the path and become a monk to learn Buddhism. It is also beneficial to ask a Zen monk about the meaning of life and of death – you should know about these things at normal times."

*The Book of Samurai*

Do not worry if you have ever been confused by the concept of karma; so were many ancient masters and so are many modern scholars. Part of the problem is that no one fully agrees on what karma actually is or how it works.

The first thing to understand about karma is that it is not exclusively Buddhist; it is a concept shared by many of India's religions, including early religions that predate Buddhism. So the concept has a very long history, and the Buddha was simply drawing upon and adapting a philosophy that was already available to him.

The word karma means "deeds" or "actions", yet the significance of the term is more to do with the results of your deeds than the deeds themselves. What is agreed among believers in karma is that your actions and intentions have consequences that will affect your future. However, some groups believe that these consequences will play out in the life you have now, whereas others believe that your deeds determine the type of rebirth that you will have. In the latter version, the karma attaches to your soul as you progress from one life to the next (although there is also a debate in Buddhism as to whether there is such a thing as a soul). Some Buddhists believe that you have to work through all of your karma before you can move to *nirvana*; others believe that the moment you reach enlightenment, all of your karma is expunged as you are freed from this existence through the Great Realization.

Having acknowledged all these different interpretations, we are left with a simple – but not simplistic – understanding of karma: that the intent behind any actions you take will leave a bill for you to pay in the future, and that good thoughts and actions will reduce your bill and bad actions will add to it.

**Follow the principle of karma: have good intentions and do good deeds. This will not only make you a better person in the present but will improve your situation in the future – whether in this life or the next.**

## Lesson 25. Ask yourself why you want to practise Zen

It is most likely that by now you will have plenty of questions about issues such as enlightenment, the afterlife and the purpose of this life and its meaning. But you are probably not searching for answers to these questions with the same level of determination and dedication as the Buddha did. Which is OK. Neither am I. I also doubt you feel like you are about to become enlightened, and so you will probably have recognized that your journey has quite some distance left to run.

So, then, if we know – or strongly suspect – that we are not going to achieve liberation in this lifetime, why bother practising Zen? Perhaps you are less interested in the ultimate goal of *nirvana* than in finding some short-term peace. Simply asking why you want to engage with Zen is a lesson in itself. But before we answer the question of just *why* we practise Zen, let us think about what we mean by enlightenment. Understanding what enlightenment is will help us understand why we might want to pursue it and what this has to do with the way of the sword, if anything at all.

**Be honest about your true reasons for practising Zen. It is nice to tell yourself that you are striding out on a path toward a grand spiritual goal, but, in truth, you may just be looking for peace of mind and a brief escape from the drudgery of daily life.**

## Lesson 26. Understand enlightenment

"Be aware that having an understanding of the principle of the path to enlightenment may make death less ominous."

### The Book of Samurai

In some forms of Buddhism followers become enlightened by considering the impermanence of human existence or by meditating on the concept of emptiness, while other systems use cosmic diagrams known as mandalas as a focus for contemplation. In Zen, on the other hand, a meditation master guides students out of their delusion, testing them along the way with questions known as koans and interviews as they pass through various stages of enlightenment. Historically, these so-called masters offered certificates for each life-changing realization, a practice I am not sure the Buddha would have approved of. Even in the days of the samurai, some considered this system of enlightenment certification to be a profiteering racket, which it most likely was. The Japanese monk and ex-samurai Suzuki Shosan (1579–1655) observed:

"These days when someone has a small experience of *satori* they set themselves up as a teacher and give certificates to others … if they would just practise as intensively and reach truer *kensho*, like the Buddha or the patriarchs, they would attain their first real level of understanding."

This quote uses two different words for enlightenment: *satori* (悟り) and *kensho* (見性). *Kensho* means "seeing your own nature", while *satori* means "realization". The suggestion here is perhaps that a lack of self-knowledge on the part of some Zen teachers causes them to exploit their "small experience of *satori*" for personal gain.

The English term "enlightenment" itself has various con-notations and its meaning has evolved over the centuries. It is first recorded in the late fourteenth century, with the sense of removing darkness from the eyes or becoming aware of something. In the mid-seventeenth century it becomes closely associated with the idea of scientific knowledge triumphing over superstition. In fact, at this time the term became shorthand in the West for moving away from unquestioning faith in God and focusing instead on observable scientific principles – a movement that became known as the Age of Enlightenment.

It was not until the 1860s that enlightenment started to be used to denote a spiritual awakening. In the West, this phenomenon had previously been referred to as illumination not enlightenment. What makes things confusing is that the terms illumination and enlightenment appear to swap meanings at this time. Just as enlightenment is taking on a spiritual connotation, illumination begins to be used as a revelation of factual truth. Therefore, it is best when talking about spiritual awakening to tread carefully and make sure that you and whoever you are conversing with have the same understanding of terms such as illumination and enlightenment.

In the previous lesson we asked what use Zen is if you cannot realistically expect to become fully enlightened in this lifetime. In Zen there is a clearly defined end goal, yet this end goal is unobtainable for most people. So what is the point of even trying? For some people, the answer to this question might be that Zen meditation can offer clarity of mind, higher cognitive functioning and better mental health in the here and now, all leading to a more fulfilling life. The world presents us with so many difficulties, and even first-world problems are still problems; the mind can be as befuddled in a five-star holiday resort as it is in the dankest of slums, or as contented on a ramshackle trailer park as it is in a luxury castle.

It is, above all, our mind and not our circumstances that creates our experience of life, and Zen is a way to break any mental chains that may be holding us back. No matter if you are a swordsman or a spiritual seeker or both, meditation is the key to clarity of mind. Left unmaintained, your mind may become worn and break down. Whatever path you are on, you will need a sharp mind and proper perception. Later we will talk of polishing the mind-mirror and explore mental maintenance, but, for now, let us celebrate, rather than question, the willingness of Zen seekers to tread a path despite not knowing whether they will ever reach its end. A noble venture by any measure.

**Aim to find moments of clarity and true happiness, with the hope that through training you can extend these moments and make them more frequent.**

## Lesson 27. Meditate on koans

There are many ways to come to spiritual experience: through prayer, contemplation, intellectual discourse, investigation, rigorous training, starvation, exhaustion, trance, devotion – people have used all such ways. However, meditation and the koan (公案) are Zen's primary avenues.

Meditation we have covered, but koans need some explanation. These perplexing, unfathomable stories, dialogues, questions and statements originated in China, where they were called *gong an* – "public statements" or "sayings". There are entire books, both old and new, dedicated to the deciphering of koans, but to attempt to understand a koan is to miss the point. Of the approximately 1,700 traditional koans to exist, none of them is meant to be answered in a logical way. Instead, they are to be absorbed and meditated upon until the mind enters a different state. The point of koans is that they are irrational and unanswerable. It is the pondering of the question that is important, not the answer. If the mind focuses long and hard enough on a single point, it will attain a new level of realization and that is what koans are for. A koan should not be deconstructed and broken down, it should be broken *through*.

This is akin to sword training: dedicated practice leading to a progression that is not a conscious action. As with sword skills, the aspirant should react subconsciously after countless hours of perseverance. The only difference is that the koan offers purely mental training, whereas the way of the sword has a physical aspect. Swordsmanship, meditation and the koan are about pushing the mind to break its form and release its inner clarity. As a result, you will develop a hypersensitive understanding of the world around you. Colours, smells, feelings are all super-enlarged and super-charged and normal experience becomes naturally euphoric, even for just a short time.

**Liberate yourself from the limitations of logicality. Some things just need to be experienced, not understood.**

# Lesson 28. Harmonize with the Way

"If you seek for something in accordance with the Way, it will be obtained without fail. This is the virtue of the Way."

*The Book of Samurai*

The Chinese character for the Dao or the Way (道) means "path" or "street". It has no special connotations in itself, but it later took on a spiritual meaning as the underlying structure-intelligence of the universe. Whether you are handling a sword or practising Zen, you will make progress by harmonizing with the Way rather than struggling against it.

The Buddha, when he was at the very end of his path just before he became enlightened and stepped out of the cycle of reincarnation, looked back and gave us a roadmap to follow. This has become associated with the Dao. But did you know that the Way is not actually a Buddhist concept? The idea of the great path comes from Chinese Daoism. As Buddhism travelled across China before it landed in Japan, the concept of the Way entered into Buddhist thought.

Lao Tzu, the author of the Dao de Jing, the central text of Daoism, is often quoted as saying "the Way that can be named is not the correct way" – but this did not stop him writing a whole book about the Way in which he contradictorily and constantly attempted to describe it. In his famous quote, Lao Tzu is not saying that the Way cannot be discussed; what he means is that the Way cannot be fully comprehended by humans, no matter what words are used. Cultures around the world have developed different ideas of "God", which they defend against rival conceptions of the universal creator, but what Daoism has above all of them is that it admits its fallibility. Daoism knows that it does not know what is at the heart of the universe, and that it cannot know the secrets beyond the veil of life. We say that "God works in mysterious ways"; Lao Tzu tells us that the secrets of the universe are incomprehensible but that we name them the Dao.

The Way should not be confused with the laws of physics, yet it does not contradict them. Physics is a human way of comprehending the observable workings of reality. Scientific discoveries can help you understand the nature of a distant star or the construction of life at the microscopic level. In contrast, the Way, the foundation upon which all reality lies, is unobservable and unfathomable. It governs fate, karma, purpose and destiny. Admittedly, the terms I have used are from different cultures but they are the best ones to highlight to you the difference between the scientific path and the spiritual path.

It is impossible for humans to comprehend what is beyond existence, beyond the laws of nature, but we know that there is a "beyond the universe", a "moment before time". The Way is both inside and outside of existence. It is the structure outside of reality that enables reality to form. Do not look for a description of the Way. Instead understand that the Way is the Alpha and the Omega; it is what comes before time and what shall remain after time. It is in command, it is never wrong, it is omnipotent and omnipresent. The Way gave you the spark of life; it is the reason why Earth is established perfectly for life, neither too hot nor too cold; and it is the reason why you are where you are right now. The Way is beyond time; it can outwait you and outthink you; it knows when you are wrong, even when you do not know it yourself, and it knows where we will all end up. It waits for you to arrive at the correct place before offering you another fork in the road. Take as many wrong turns as you like, the universe can wait. Call it God, the Dao, the universe, the creator, it does not matter. No religion can describe what is beyond reality, try as it might. Lao Tzu fully realized this truth and he called it the Way because it holds a path for each and every one of us. Each path is unique, but they all ultimately lead to the same place, true realization and enlightenment. This is where the Buddha ended up, and we could do too … eventually.

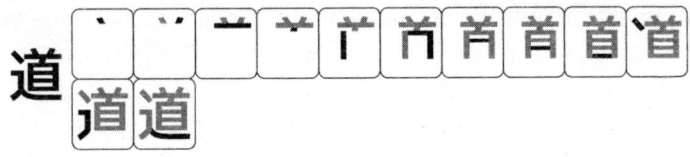

The previous *kanji* image introduced us to the Chinese character for the Way (道), but now it is time to focus on it more closely. The character is constructed of the head of a human who is walking down a winding path. It implies that you are wandering along the great path set out for you by the universe.

**Always, always remember that you are not waiting for the universe, the universe is waiting for you. Move in harmony with the Way and you will progress.**

## Lesson 29. Know that there are ways as well as the Way

We have seen that, used on its own, the Chinese character for the Way (道) represents the indescribable laws that underpin the universe. However, this character can also be used in combination with other characters to refer to a philosophical approach to a particular subject or pursuit. You may have heard of: *chado* (茶道), the way of tea; *shodo* (書道), the way of calligraphy; *kado* (華道), the way of flower arrangement; and maybe even *kodo* (香道), the way of fragrance. If you are interested in Japanese martial arts, you will almost certainly know: *kendo* (剣道), the way of the sword; *iaido* (居合道), the way of quick drawing the sword; and *judo* (柔道), the way of flexible fighting. Why then is the Dao used in these two different forms: as the universal Way and as earthly ways?

To attempt an answer to this this question, let us return to reincarnation. It is one of the more persuasive aspects of afterlife theory, in that it offers one explanation for why people are born into such different circumstances with different abilities and attitudes, and why not everyone arrives at the same spiritual realizations before death. It appears to take many turns of the wheel of *samsara* before an individual reaches the end of their existence. In the meantime, we need a focus to keep our minds from wandering off the path of Heaven, and these smaller ways give us just that. The way of calligraphy, the way of tea, the way of Zen, or even the way of the warrior, give us focus. You can learn multiple ways across a lifetime or you can dedicate yourself to just one.

**Once you have understood that the Way is the nature behind the universe, the next step is to find a way to fulfil its expectations of you. Sampling a variety of experiences can be enriching but it does not match lifelong dedication to a single focus. By all means search around, but when you find your passion devote yourself to it entirely.**

## Lesson 30. Follow the four great paths which become one

The four great paths of Japanese religious tradition are Buddhism, Confucianism, Daoism and Shinto. Daoism is often not listed among the religions of Japan but it is prevalent throughout the country's culture. These four strands were all originally intertwined but over millennia they have frayed out in different directions. However, each one complements the others by regulating a certain aspect of our earthly or spiritual existence:

- Buddhism focuses on your inner mind and spiritual progression.
- Confucianism controls how you behave in society.
- Daoism deals with the universe, its creation and your place in it.
- Shinto is the way to connect to the past and the realm of the gods.

Taken together, these four religious traditions allow you to interact with the world, society, history and the spiritual realm with a proper attitude. Your task is to investigate each one and integrate it into your being. For further details on doing this, see lesson 94 of *How to Be a Modern Samurai*, which is the companion to this book.

**Take advantage of living in the information age. All faiths and cultures are open to us and we no longer have to stick with the religion of our ancestors if we do not want to. The dogma and indoctrination of organized religion is crumbling, leaving behind the true teachings for us to gather up.**

## Lesson 31. Recognize the way of the warrior as the lowest path

"Weapons are the instruments of ill-omen; all decent humans detest them … and their use except in the greatest need."

Dao de Jing

When reading ancient holy texts, it becomes obvious that the way of the warrior is viewed as the lowest of all the spiritual paths. Most religions are fundamentally opposed to weapons and war. However, almost all of them find a way to reconcile themselves to violence. The samurai were no different: they distinguished between justifiable and unjustifiable wars and, on a personal level, they meted out what they considered to be justifiable violence with the "life-giving sword" (whereas unjustifiable violence was condemned as having been delivered by the "death-dealing sword"). It goes to show that people have always found a means of reframing their actions to show themselves in a favourable light.

As an aspiring Zen warrior, you have to understand that to choose the way of the sword means to take the lowest path. But this is still a high road. You are still on *the* path. You can discover the practical way of violence through the sword as a means to train your body and become a proficient swordsman while channelling the calmness of Zen. Alternatively, you can use swordsmanship as a medium of meditation, a way to engage with Zen. The latter, of course, is not effective in combat, but if combat is not your aim then it is a good option.

**If you follow the way of the sword, do not expect to be loved or respected. Societies have not always valued their warriors ... until they need them.**

# Lesson 32. Rediscover the beginner's mind

"In reality, if you fight with someone with a sword with the resolution to kill them, two or three tenths of your attack is substantial, which is that which you can control, while seven or eight tenths is insubstantial – which is that which you cannot control."

*The Book of Ninja*

When someone untrained in combat is attacked with violence, they will defend themselves naturally. Likewise, someone untrained in painting will just paint away happily, and the writer with no idea of structure will free-flow their ideas on to the page, creating story after story. In Zen, this is known as *shoshin* (初心), the beginner's mind. The moment a person begins to study form, rules, tactics, techniques and so on, they start to fixate on those structures and lose touch with what they would do naturally. This stops the person from being free mentally. Are my feet in the correct place? Am I holding the sword or the brush correctly? Should I move before or after the opponent? The mind stops at these questions. Thus, the beginner's mind is highly sought after by Zen masters.

Why, then, would anyone want to engage in training if the mind with which they start out is the best mind to have? The answer is simple: because you would be terrible at your chosen art if you did not practise it. The beginner's mind is an attitude that experts want to cultivate, but it is separate from their level of ability. A painter with zero training or experience will create terrible pictures; a writer who does not understand how to develop a story will write drivel; while an untrained fighter will die in their first real sword fight. The beginner acts in a free-flowing manner, but their execution is poor. What you are aiming for is to become so well trained in the finer points of your craft that you no longer have to think about them. Then you will be able to return to that beginner's mind, which is fluid and dynamic and free.

**To master any skill, combine the ability of an expert with the mental freedom of a complete beginner.**

## Lesson 33. Do your duty

"The primary principle that samurai should keep in mind during daily life is: 'During a state of order you should consider and prepare for war and in a time of disorder you should think for the best way to bring about peace.'"

*The Book of Samurai*

Japanese society, particularly in former times, and particularly among the samurai, has always been known for a strong sense of duty. *Bushi* were military men paid a salary for ensuring that they were in a constant state of readiness for war. Unfortunately, military service no longer works that way. Imagine if the army paid you to stay at home training yourself and your children and that is all you had to do. You would, of course, feel duty bound to the army. In their intense dutifulness, the samurai were very different from most of us, and this begs the question, where do *you* place your duty?

For the Japanese there are various forms of duty. The first is known as *on* (恩), the duty you owe to people who have bestowed benefits upon you; then there is *giri* (義理), which refers to social and legal obligations, a reciprocal network that holds society together. Much of this stems from Confucian philosophy, which became particularly influential in the latter part of the samurai era.

If you want to follow a samurai approach to duty, consider what cause you might choose to dedicate yourself to. This could be a faith, an organization, an ideal, a mission. You must also take seriously your obligation to control your behaviour in society. But not only that, you should feel genuine happiness and gratitude for all the good things you have in your life and pay off your debts, financial or otherwise.

**Follow the samurai example by finding a worthy cause to dedicate yourself to, something that is greater than your own needs. Make sure that your actions have a positive, not negative, effect on society.**

## Lesson 34. Choose a sword and a cushion

"Once you are given a *tachi* by the lord, you should not carry it without bathing it in blood. However, if you are in a position of commanding a number of people, you cannot fight for yourself, which means that you cannot bathe the sword in blood. Therefore, you should decline the sword."

*The Book of Samurai*

Two things you will need on your path to becoming a Zen warrior are a sword and a cushion. The sword you will wield to train your body, while the cushion you will sit on to train your mind.

A good sword is essential. Of course, cost may be an issue and you must live within your means. For those on a tighter budget, I would suggest investing in a decent wooden Japanese sword. It is better to buy a high-quality wooden sword than a poor-quality steel one. Almost all of my personal training is done with a wooden sword.

If you are new to buying swords, be aware that there are three basic categories of steel sword:

1. Antique Japanese swords. These are generally the most expensive and are hard to obtain, depending on which country you live in. Therefore, you will not want to damage them and so they may not be the best option to use as a practical sword.
2. Replica swords. Although these are modern made, they can be used as functioning *katana* and are a good option.
3. Display swords. These have zero practical use. Avoid at all costs.

I have all three types, but now I favour my wooden sword for its practicality and my antique steel sword for its sacredness.

The length of the sword is also something to bear in mind. The Japanese say that your sword blade should be ten fists long. The ten-fist sword is one of Japan's most ancient traditions. Early Japanese swords tended to be *tachi*, or great swords, long, two-handed weapons which were used on the open battlefield and on horseback. However, by the time Zen became closely associated with the sword, the shorter *katana* had taken over.

Japanese Zen practitioners always use a cushion to meditate on. Many Westerners do not, and consequently receive a numb bum as a reward. Therefore, find a cushion that will be comfortable for you to sit on for long periods. You might consider buying a traditional Japanese meditation cushion known as a *zafu*. These are round and designed to raise your hips, which helps to make the classic cross-legged meditation position more accessible and comfortable, particularly for those with restricted flexibility.

Other points to consider as an adherent of Zen include your appearance and your surroundings. You should be clean and neat and wear clothes that are simple and practical, and you should keep your home well-ordered, tidy and free-flowing. By maintaining yourself and your environment in an orderly state, you will be better equipped to deal with everything life throws at you with equanimity.

**Buy less, but buy better. Be wary of brand names and logos, but instead search out well-made, visually pleasing, functional items.**

## Lesson 35. Be aware of the scientific–supernatural argument

Throughout this book we will explore scientific and supernatural interpretations of aspects of Zen and, in some ways, help to align them. One of the main arguments that you should be aware of is over whether Zen states of mind have a supernatural origin or whether they are just ancient ways of describing how the human brain works for everyone. Is "no-mind" another way of describing the unconscious mind, or the subconscious mind, or is it a mystical state accessible only to true Zen masters? Is the famous Zen self-control related to the Western psychological hypothesis of hot and cold cognition, which examines the effect of emotion on reasoning. When a Zen practitioner has a meditative breakthrough, is this caused by a supernatural intervention or by a chemical change in the brain? There are no definitive answers to be found here, only the identification of the argument. All you have to do is be aware of it.

**Your body is bound by the scientifically established laws of nature. However, do not limit your reach by thinking too much about the restrictions of science. Your experience is your own; only you can control how far you push it.**

## Lesson 36. Challenge yourself to the warrior's quest

"Facing off with a sword-like heart is a tradition where you should speak with determination and to the point – this is to externally display your 'inner blade'. If you do not have such determination then it is best to avoid saying words of grave importance."

*The Book of Samurai*

To test their ability, Zen monks would set out on a spiritual pilgrimage called an *angya* (行脚), during which they would engage in Zen contests against other monks. Likewise, *musha-shugyo* (武者修行) is the tradition of *bushi* taking to the road to test their skills away from their normal lives, especially in sacred spaces. *Bushi* would also perform *tanren* (鍛錬), which was hardcore training that ranged from 100 to 1,000 days.

Contrary to popular belief, not all sword duels in samurai times were to the death. In fact, duels to the death were outlawed around the year 1600 and often fighting was similar to modern-day sports championships. This meant that the potential consequences of challenging an opponent to a fight were less drastic than in earlier times (although, of course, some fights did still result in death). Good fighters became popular; likewise, a monk who had achieved successes within Zen was known as a "man of the sword".

Testing one's skill level is central to both Zen practice and sword craft. Likewise, *you* must test yourself in the world. This could be through friendly sword bouts, or through debating groups – anything that pushes you beyond your normal boundaries or compels you to face your fears. Such things must be done. However, they must be done in the correct way without pride and without a destructive attitude.

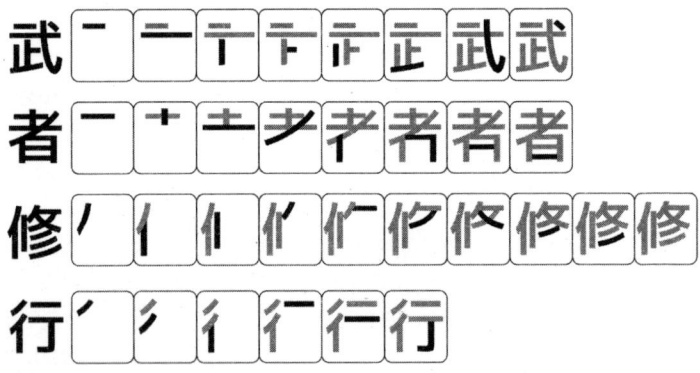

The characters for *musha-shugyo* (武者修行) mean "the warrior who travels to attain his qualifications".

**Always look for opportunities to engage in your chosen path, rather than excuses not to. You can outwait your own life, but you cannot outwait the universe. It is waiting for you to get off your backside and do something.**

## Round-up

We have now finished the first leg of our journey and have reached a place where your mind should be free of misconceptions. So far we have discussed the basic outline of Zen and the *bushi*, and how to avoid the pitfalls of language and problems with translation. You now have a starting point for practising Japanese calligraphy, for engaging with the Japanese sword, and understanding the human brain. We have explored together the cultural treasure of the samurai, and looked at Zen's journey from India, through China, to Japan. You now know that a connection exists between Zen and violence, but that you should anchor yourself in the four great spiritual paths of the East. You can also prepare yourself to practise *zazen* meditation and try to fathom koans, karma and karmic debt, to know that you are striving for realization on your way toward enlightenment, something which will not happen in this lifetime but which is the end goal for your soul. You now know to understand the sword as a holy item and a status symbol but remain focused on its practicality. But above all you should maintain the mind of the beginner and simply choose for yourself the meditation cushion or the sword – or both. All of this has been your first step on the Zen warrior's quest and it is time to move on to the second part of your journey.

# PART 2.
# ESTABLISH A FORM

This part of your journey will help you develop body and mind, and hopefully your attitude to training, with the aim of perfecting all of these. One of the first things you will learn is that you do not have to wait to delve into deeper realms of Zen philosophy, nor wait before engaging in higher-level sword training. However, it is equally important not to over-intellectualize Zen. Avoid the trap of talking Zen but not doing Zen. We will also cover some Chinese concepts such as the four ways to approach life that influenced Zen as it passed through China. We will look at physiological issues such as eye function and muscle memory that have particular relevance to sword training and discuss the importance of *kata* and forms in your training. This takes us to the question of where and how to train, including the ongoing debate about the usefulness of sparring and full-contact combat. Turning from the body to the mind, we will explore desire, attachment and correct mind. Lastly, we will touch on the Buddha-mind, the end goal of all Zen.

## Lesson 37. Practise, practise, practise

"When studying an art, start slowly and carefully and when the 'fire' ignites within, study with intensity. This is the path to excellence."

### The Book of Samurai

There is an ongoing debate as to how experts are created. How much is down to repetition and practice, and how much is down to natural ability? According to a commonly cited theory, practising a particular skill the right way for 10,000 hours can make an expert of anyone, regardless of their natural talent. However, others firmly believe that true mastery can only be achieved by those who start out with an innate gift. Other factors cited as important include beginning at a young age, and having an encouraging family background and access to the best facilities and coaching.

Of course, the very greatest exponents of a particular skill will generally have most, if not all, of these factors working in their favour, particularly dedication and natural talent. Someone with talent who does not put in the hours of training will never fully realize their potential; someone of lesser ability who trains hard will most likely go beyond their potential.

The conclusion? Training is the key to improvement, regardless of your level of natural ability. So practise, practise and practise again.

**Practise and study your chosen subject, but practise it more than you study it. Also, be aware that study involves more than just reading books; it means breaking down your subject over and over again and rebuilding your understanding of it.**

## Lesson 38. Find a place to train

In the modern world, space is often a luxury. This was also a problem for some samurai. Before the samurai moved into the cities, most lived on their own farming estates with room aplenty. However, as the wars came to an end the samurai slowly started to move into the cities near to the major castle. They no longer had enough space of their own in which to develop their martial arts skills and so they had to attend the "sports halls" of their day. Luckily, *zazen* meditation does not take much room to perform; you just need to sit down. Swordsmanship, on the other hand, does need space.

Consider the following options when deciding where to carry out your own sword training. Some of these suggestions are inspired by the settings in which the samurai used to train. Also bear in mind, of course, that training is best done with a partner if you have one.

### In a personal space

A converted garage or room can be turned into a simple *dojo*. Often ceiling height is the problem not floor dimensions as you need a lot of room to swing a sword above your head.

### In a public building

The samurai government of the Edo period saw that samurai needed places to train and so purpose-built halls were provided in most cities. Samurai could go to a Tuesday afternoon *jujutsu* class and do flower arranging in the next room on a Thursday, followed by a Saturday morning sword class and so on. Enquire about local village halls, town sports centres or any other recreational spaces that can be hired.

### On spiritual ground

Often *bushi* would take themselves off to train in temples, where they could practise martial arts in combination with Zen. They might also practise at Shinto shrines or take pilgrimages to holy mountains or other natural sacred spaces within the landscape. Training outside in a natural setting offers a specific advantage over indoor *dojo* training: it accustoms you to combat on uneven terrain. As the renowned swordsman Miyamoto Musashi warns us, *bushi* have to be able to fight in all sorts of conditions.

**Explore your area to find spaces where you can engage in practice. There may be a perfect place nearby. The question is, have you looked?**

## Lesson 39. Learn how your eyes work

"By paying attention with your eyes and mind, you can attain your own achievements and win battles. Remember, observing with perception is different from seeing."
*The Book of Samurai*

In sword combat, you need all your senses to be finely tuned, none more so than your eyesight. Historical samurai arts speak of various ways to use observation and eye gaze when in combat, which we will cover more deeply in lesson 71. However, before then we will look in general terms at the way our field of vision is divided into different sectors and how high-stress combat situations can affect the way the eyes function.

The typical human field of vision across both eyes is an oval shape that extends approximately 95 degrees to each side of a central point, and 60 degrees above and 75 degrees below that central point. The central area is where focus is sharpest, but things gradually become more blurred as your view widens. The sharply focused zone directly ahead of you is called foveal vision, named after the fovea, which is the part of the retina that specializes in highly detailed observation. Anything outside of the foveal area is referred to as peripheral vision. This is divided into three concentric bands: the near peripheral, which is just outside the central foveal area; the mid peripheral; and the far peripheral, which is at the edge of our field of vision.

In normal times, the foveal and peripheral work together to give us a balanced field of vision that provides a combination of focus and range. However, during intense combat situations requiring heightened awareness, our adrenaline levels spike and this triggers a shift in balance from the peripheral to the foveal. Our eyes switch to a form of tunnel vision as our gaze fixates on our opponent.

We also benefit from a phenomenon called the vestibulo-ocular reflex, which enables us to maintain a steady gaze even when we are making the kind of sudden head movements that are typical in sword combat.

In short, your eyes do not always act in the same way but will move between vision types and focus depending on the situation.

**Appreciate your eyes and look after them. They are a miracle of natural engineering.**

## Lesson 40. Train your muscle memory

Typing on a keyboard, tying shoelaces, returning a tennis serve, driving a car, playing a computer game and parrying a sword have one thing in common: they are physical tasks we can learn to do largely without thinking by training our long-term muscle memory.

The part of the brain that governs muscle memory is called the cerebellum, a term believed to have been coined by Leonardo da Vinci in the early sixteenth century. The cerebellum accounts for only 10 per cent of brain volume but holds more than half of the brain's nerve cells. Among these are the Purkinje cells, named after Dr Johannes Purkinje who discovered them in the 1830s, which play a vital part in coordination, control and the learning of movements – the components of muscle memory, in other words. The cerebellum is a true powerhouse at the back of the skull. In Paul MacLean's three-layer theory of the brain (see lesson 5), the cerebellum is part of the deepest layer, the so-called reptilian brain, which controls instinctive, unconscious behaviour and actions. Conscious behaviour is handled by the cerebrum, the largest part of the brain, which is situated outside the cerebellum at the top and front of the head.

In any situation your brain can make war with itself; the conscious mind can fight to take control over the unconscious mind and a person can become stuck between the two, a problem known as "stopping" to medieval Japanese swordsmen (see lesson 60). While both conscious and unconscious minds are useful in high-speed interactions, the unconscious mind is the better one to use as it reacts more quickly.

Author and researcher Christopher Bergland uses the term "superfluidity" to describe when an athlete's movements derive entirely from unconscious reactions that have been programmed by muscle memory. The key to success is having the muscles make the correct reactions. If someone tries to poke you in the eye and you blink, jerk your head to the side, lose your balance and stumble over the sofa, your reaction is certainly unconscious but it is also untrained. Simply moving out of poking range would be a more trained reaction. Jumping out of the way of a bus, swatting a fly, swerving or braking to avoid a car crash are all situations where the unconscious mind takes over and where no conscious decisions are actually made; it is only afterwards that we piece together what happened.

Often when we are driving, our minds switch to autopilot and we arrive at our destination but never remember making the turns or seeing other cars; we just know we arrived but have no idea who made all the decisions to get us there safely. We are able to control a large metal object moving at high speed in close proximity to hundreds of other speeding metal objects controlled by other people and all these people are able to avoid colliding with each other (most of the time) and to do all this without even thinking. This is an example of superfluidity in action and it is the perfect mindset for combat. Ancient masters of the sword would see this as a divine accomplishment. Every time you drive and sing along to your favourite music, play tennis with ease, type an email, text on your phone, play a computer game, or anything that you have trained yourself to do with ease, you are engaging in what ancient masters considered the greatest skill. Now imagine if you practise with a sword for as long as you have surfed the web or driven a car. That is the only difference between you and the masters of old.

**Repeat the movements and techniques of sword combat over and over and over until you can do them without thinking.**

## Lesson 41. Practise using *waza* and *kata*

In Japanese martial arts training, *waza* (技) are individual techniques or skills and *kata* (型) are combinations of prescribed movements. It can be said that a *kata* is, in fact, a collection of *waza* combined. Both *waza* and *kata* are repeated thousands of times to imprint different responses on the body's muscle memory. The job of your brain is to identify the correct response for each situation. *Waza* can be compared to chess moves. Each chess piece has its own way of moving, and good chess players are able to combine these individual patterns to build a path to victory. *Kata* are often performed in pairs as a kind of physical dialogue between training partners who work together to hone their unconscious reactions. They basically agree to a staged fight to help them practise.

Some martial arts practitioners have questioned the usefulness of *kata*, arguing that too much choreographing of movements can lead to predictability and embed bad habits in the muscle memory. The nineteenth-century sword master Yamaoka Tesshu considered *kata* to be a dead method. Instead, he would imagine an opponent in front of him and play out combat in his mind. This he called *muteki no kyokusho* ("against no enemy") and it formed a fundamental aspect of his swordsmanship.

Observing other, more experienced practitioners can also be a good way to improve your own abilities. The brain is believed to contain mirror neurons, which are activated when we watch someone else performing an action and help us to replicate the movement. However, regular practice is the key to success. Reading and watching will get you only so far. Pick up your sword and practise, practise, practise.

**Build up a collection of mental and physical responses. Assess them as you go along, keeping the ones that help you most and throwing out any that do not help you.**

## Lesson 42. Decide whether to spar

To spar or not to spar is *the* great debate in the world of martial arts. Advocates of sparring argue that without pitting yourself against an opponent as part of your training you can never properly test your own skills. On the other hand, those who favour individual training would say that sparring in a controlled environment with safety rules and no danger of death does not allow the inner mind to take control. They argue that the whole point of practising forms and skill sets so rigorously is to train the mind and muscle memory to go into activation mode when life-threatening danger arises.

Returning to the teachings of Yamaoka Tesshu (see previous lesson), he believed that light sparring or matches between students had almost no benefit. However, he himself engaged in prolonged sparring sessions called *shujitsu kazu shiai*. The gruelling challenge he set himself was to face 200 sparring partners a day, non-stop, for seven days in succession, a total of 1,400 bouts. His reasoning was that only after so much sparring would the unconscious mind take over and a sense of genuine combat be created. As we have seen, Yamaoka also disapproved of *kata* and formal patterns. He engaged in a form of training known as *gedan jiai*, which is a particular form of light sparring where each swordsman keeps the hilt of their sword in a lowered position while they attempt to strike or block their opponent. The purpose of this is to stop students from swinging high and wild, something that is commonly seen in sports but does not stand up in life-threatening situations.

To help you reach a verdict in the great sparring debate, consider the following three options:

1. **Practise sword forms only**. If you do this enthusiastically and with an edge of realism, you can hope that you will imprint the moves on your muscle memory and that your unconscious mind will know what to do when danger arises.
2. **Enter into half combat with a partner**, a form of free-flowing training that is more structured than full-contact sparring. It is a shared exploration of the way the body and the sword move and is designed to promote the development of muscle memory.
3. **Engage in full-contact sparring** in the hope that your body will begin to react in the correct way to fast, unstructured aggression.

**Periodically check that your training methods are giving you the results you want. Do not stick with a method that you feel is not helping you, but make sure you give it enough time before you decide to abandon it.**

## Lesson 43. Adapt to the situation

Your mind should be trained to switch between four basic ways, known collectively as *shido*. Do this with conscious thought and effort. The four ways are:

1. Flexibility, known as *ju* (柔)
2. Rigidity, known as *go* (剛)
3. Strength, known as *kyo* (強)
4. Softness, known as *jyaku* (弱).

These are actually two sets of opposing pairs which have been known since before the time of the *bushi* and come to us from ancient China. It is up to you to determine which of the four states is needed in each situation. Dealing with the world can be stressful and the correct use of these four aspects can reduce confrontation in your life. For example, if someone is trying to make you do something that you do not really mind doing and will cause you no problems, be flexible. However, if it is something that will cause you problems in the future, remain rigid in your position.

Be aware of the difference between strength and rigidity, as they can be easily confused. With strength you become overbearing, powerful and dominant, and make a forward move. Rigidity, on the other hand, is to simply stand your ground – not pushing forward but not moving back.

The difference between flexibility and softness is that with flexibility you adapt to a situation, become wily, manoeuvre your conversation or position well, whereas with softness you just give in to being dominated, at least for a short time, until you can change the situation you are in.

Learn to consciously move between these states and to do it at the correct time. Know when to give ground and when to stand your ground, when to push forward and when to retreat. This will make for a smoother more stress-free life.

**Be adaptable, but know that adaptability does not mean always being submissive. Samurai strategy tells us to take no**

action most of the time, but to take action when it is needed. To do nothing when you should act is a failure, but so is to do something when you should do nothing.

## Lesson 44. Master the three-layered approach

The basis of your whole venture onto the Zen warrior path is to attain the most organized and focused mind you can achieve on your way to higher realization. Now you must consider how to approach your study and to become an expert in your chosen field. The *bushi* referred to this approach as *shuhari* (守破離). The word breaks down into three distinct components: *shu*, *ha* and *ri*. *Shu* (守) is to stick strictly to the fundamentals, to follow the basics and not deviate until you have mastered them. *Ha* (破) is to start to break with those basic skills, to experiment "outside of the box". This does not mean that you ignore what you have learned or try to change it; it means to start to flow freely between your skills, to use the best skill you have in your arsenal for each situation and to be able to link them together in whichever order is best to tackle the problem you are facing. The final stage of the approach, *ri* (離), is to break away and create something new from the building blocks of your skills. At this point, you have full mastery and knowledge of your subject. Not only are you able to use your arts in any order so as to be fluid and flexible, but you are able to develop and introduce new ideas and skills. These will be effective because they have grown out of practical experience not untested imagination.

Consider a builder. Laying the bricks is the level of *shu*; knowing all the skills of building a conventional house is *ha*; but a true master-builder can move on to the stage of *ri* and design and build unique houses that defy conventionality and will set the standard for future builders. This is the concept of *shuhari*, the three stages of evolution, and it is the same for any art.

**Build your study on firm foundations. Master the basics so that you can call upon a reservoir of knowledge and skills instantly. This will enable you to progress to the higher levels with confidence.**

## Lesson 45. Do not wait to create your masterpiece

Be aware of what I call the "Japanese spell". This is the same spell that Merlin has over us, that of the wise old sage who appears as the perfect guide. The truth is, according to one samurai writing, a *bushi* needed no more than seven years to become fully trained. Therefore, many samurai would have been ready for battle by the end of their teenage years. You should erase the image of the greying, aged martial arts master from your imagination and replace it with the young, athletic samurai, hot blooded, bold and hungry for adventure.

Stop looking ahead to the completion of your training at the end of a long life and understand that training is the whole point of the path you are trying to walk down. Do not be the artist who "one day" will create their masterpiece; sketch now and keep sketching, then in time you will realize that you have already created your masterpiece. Age on its own does not bring wisdom; wisdom comes above all from effort.

Do not put off approaching a complex question, or anything that seems beyond your comprehension. Now is the time to engage with such matters so that one day you will fulfil the archetype of the wise advisor for other people on the same path as you. You can become King Arthur and Merlin rolled into one, an active expert and a perfect guide.

**Seize this moment to grapple with the most profound questions. They are not reserved for better, cleverer people, the mysterious "others", to deal with; these challenges are laid before you so that you can progress. Now is the time for you to rise to your feet in effort or to sit down in meditation.**

## Lesson 46. Do not intellectualize Zen

Let us now return to Zen. Zen and education are somewhat at odds with each other. Zen adepts are meant to follow the path of experience until they reach various stages of realization. However, over the years, as Zen established centres of control and extended its influence into politics, higher learning and Zen practice became entwined with each other. This leads us to a problem. To follow Zen is to disentangle oneself from worldly matters, to observe life from the wanderer's viewpoint. The ideal approach is based purely on practical experience – the Buddha's way, if you like. However, throughout its history Zen has attracted the attention of highly educated people who have focused on the political, historical and theoretical aspects of Buddhism and Zen. This is the wrong approach, because by fixating on the complexities of religious philosophy you lose the point of Zen, which is experience.

If you have to engage with complex matters, do so in a free-flowing way. Never attach yourself to dogma and keep an open mind. It is good to have a grasp of current affairs, poetry and the arts and to cultivate a basic knowledge of general history and the nature of different religions and their history. Also develop some understanding of Zen history and philosophy. If you are focused on the way of the *bushi* then read military literature, including military classics and chronicles.

However, be aware that on this Zen path you are not a historian, a politician, a philosopher, a chronicler, a storyteller or a military commander. You are an adherent to the Zen way through the art of the Japanese sword and your focus should be on meditation, contemplation and combat with a sword. The Buddha existed before the samurai and before all the Chinese and Japanese chronicles, and he lived thousands of miles away from Japan, yet he was the one the samurai followed. As far as we know, the Buddha never studied history; he just followed the correct path. Therefore, never get bogged down in the complex web of literature and history. Zen is experience first. The proper way to gain enlightenment is through work, practice and dedication. If you want to talk about Zen, it must be at the end of hours of gruelling toil. Only then will you have earned the privilege to talk about it.

**If you talk on a subject, make sure that you talk from experience and listen to those who have more experience than you. Avoid getting bogged down in trivial arguments about history or theory.**

# Lesson 47. Develop correct mind

"With a mindset of righteousness achievement can be attained. Righteousness is where reason and truth exist and every decision should be made from the wellspring of such reason and truth."

*The Book of Samurai*

In the early to mid-seventeenth century, a Buddhist priest called Takuan Soho exchanged a series of letters with the swordsman Yagyu Munenori in which they discussed the connection between Zen and swordsmanship. This correspondence has become famous among Japanese *kenjutsu* practitioners all over the world, and one of the important themes of the dialogue, correct mindedness, has become a staple of modern swordsmanship.

The concept of the correct mind, an attitude that steers people toward wisdom, virtue, benevolence, morality and so on, occurs throughout *bushi* and Buddhist literature. Another take on the idea can be found in the writings of the warrior Hagihara Juzo, who explored situations where correct intent can motivate bad actions or positive actions can result from bad intent.

It is never a case of extinguishing your humanity and becoming emotionless and robotic; instead, samurai teachings are about not allowing emotion to cause you to react incorrectly. For example, the samurai concept known as the Dignity of the Flying Hawk means to soar above others with natural morality and inner power.

Correct mind is a subject that has a lot of weight attached to it. In short, make sure that your thoughts, words and actions are aligned in the right direction. This is the secret to correct mind.

**Know that your intention is always paramount. You may be able to conceal your true motivation from others and even from yourself, but you cannot hide any bad intention from the all-seeing universe.**

## Lesson 48. Control your desire

Controlling desire does not mean to abstain completely from anything that gives you pleasure, whether that be sex, alcohol, meat or whatever. It means to rein in your urges and to not give in to every whim. We all have habits we find it hard to resist. On the Zen warrior path you have to control both mind and body and that means identifying your desires and restraining them, *not* denying them totally.

Be careful about sticking too strictly to your principles. I have seen a situation where a former meat-eater who is now a vegetarian was mistakenly given some meat and threw it away. To my mind, the correct thing for them to have done in that moment would have been either to set aside their principles temporarily and eat the meat or to give it to someone else. Instead, good food went to waste. I did not drink alcohol between the ages of 18 and 35 and that possibly caused me more problems than if I had just drunk in moderation. Addiction slows us down or steers us down the wrong path, but desire drives us forward. Have desire, engage in pleasure, but control it strictly.

**Live your life according to guiding principles rather than hard and fast rules. Be flexible, but never allow your inner dialogue to persuade you to do something that you know in your heart is wrong.**

## Lesson 49. Cultivate non-attachment

As we have seen, attachment to anything – including people, possessions, ideas and experiences – is seen in Buddhism as a primary cause of suffering (see lesson 9). Part of your Zen warrior quest is to cultivate non-attachment. Understand that there is a difference between non-attachment and detachment. Detaching from someone or something is to be cold, alien and removed, while non-attachment is to be involved with someone or something without being dependent on them or it. Too many times I have seen samurai students try to be aloof, showing a feigned sense of having no desire, doing their best to deny normal human emotions. In fact, it is your duty as someone on the Buddhist path to engage with the world so as to spread compassion among all beings, but it is also your duty to avoid becoming too involved in the lives of others or making other people's lives your own. You cannot control other people, and you should not try to do so.

If people or things leave your life then it is neither good nor bad; it is just the way it is. Move with the flow and do the best you can in each moment. That is the secret people are looking for, but which they find too dull to be profound.

The key is to involve yourself with people but never long for them or try to force them to stay with you. Of course, you can be an organiser, you can invite friends over, you can be at the centre of a social circle or the leader of a group, but never be angry or disappointed if nothing comes of your efforts or if people do not bend to your will. Be a facilitator, not a controller.

**Accept the impermanence of all things. Some people decide to come together in a friendship or a relationship, but it is not a locked circle. If one of them wants to leave, the other must accept this. If it is time, it is time.**

## Lesson 50. Control your anger

"Have the determination not to ruin yourself by being short-tempered and do not indulge in momentary and impulsive anger."

### *The Book of Samurai*

Very few sports fighters win without having a hard edge, but they are able to stop their aggression bubbling over into anger. Anger is a powerful energy, but it can cloud your judgement and it burns out quickly. In battle, the *bushi* learned to channel their fury and bloodlust into energetic, but focused movements. Rushing here and there in a frenzy will get you tired and confused; lethal efficiency with controlled speed is the way to come out of any combat situation on top. The trick is to combine your aggression with a clear mind and focused fluidity. This will lead to grace and power in thought and movement. Maintaining this approach is the key to controlling your anger. However, staying calm does not mean being a pushover or a victim. As stated previously, you should follow the way of the hawk, which is to be filled with high stores of energy but to appear smooth and serene.

**Be slow to anger but quick to take control of threatening situations. It is difficult to control your temper, so look out for your own personal warning signs and deal with them.**

## Lesson 51. Find your Buddha-mind

One thing to always remember is that you are in fact one of the luckiest beings in the universe. Why? Because you have been born with divinity, the divine spark, and no one can remove it, no one can beat it out of you; it is unchanging, and even after you die it will still be yours. Of all the creatures on all the planets and in all the realms of life, you have been born a thinking human who has interest in your own purpose. In addition to this you are now planning for your future lives and hoping to reduce your karmic debt. This makes you one of the most special beings in all of existence, so do not waste this experience. Your quest? To find your Buddha-mind.

The Buddha-mind – sometimes known as Buddha-nature – is the foundation of your mind-stream or "soul" and it is a state to be uncovered through Zen. Thousands of hours of Zen meditation and sword training in this lifetime will not be enough to achieve this goal. But what it will do is take off layers of grime and offer you glimpses of the Buddha-mind. Forget the end goal, focus on the polishing. There are many metaphors for explaining this – a bright moon behind dark clouds, a shining jewel in the dirt, a smudged mirror to be polished, a reflection taking shape in calming waters – but no matter which you choose, the process is always the same: self-refinement. Through training and developing your wisdom, intellect and humanity, you will clear away the obstructions that lie between your human consciousness and the divine state held deeper within you. When you fail to work on your own mind or become bogged down in unhelpful thoughts, a new layer of dirt is added. It is up to you whether you do things that will improve your state or diminish it. This battle will continue for all your existences until you hit the truth that is buried deep within you.

**Moving forward is not always a progression. You can move forward in the wrong direction. Most of the time you are in a wrong state of mind; it is only when you are actively looking for truth that you get life right.**

## Round-up

We have now come to the end of part two. In this section we looked at how to develop your body and mind and your attitude to training while perfecting both. As long as you study the basics and do not over-intellectualize its philosophies then you can dive into the deep end of Zen training. We discovered how the ancient Chinese used to approach life with their four fundamental ways. We looked at the human body, how the eyes work, and the importance of muscle memory; we debated *kata* and sparring and looked at the best way to train. We ventured on to a deeper exploration of the mind by examining the concepts of desire, attachment and correct mind. Finally, we touched on the Buddha-mind and outlined the end goal for all people following the path of Zen. In the next part we will push on deeper into mental training.

# PART 3.
# HONE YOUR MIND

Having established a foundation in the last section, it is now time to hone your mind and to investigate the brain to a deeper level. In this part, we will explore the basics of brain chemistry and discuss the unconscious mind. We will also investigate the senses, including the hard-to-define sixth sense, before learning how to avoid being hampered by delusion and the mental curse of "stopping" and considering whether it is possible to penetrate our opponent's mind. Next, we will look at aspects of Zen that can benefit us mentally, including the Gateless Gate, the secrets of *mu* and *fudoshin* and the famous Ten Ox-Herding Pictures. We will also discuss what to do if your mind becomes "stained" – how to polish your mind and calm the waters of your emotions. Finally, we will take a deeper look at meditation techniques, all with the aim of accepting life and death as you set out on your path to enlightenment.

## Lesson 52. Understand basic brain chemistry

In previous lessons, we have looked at the structure of the brain. Now we will turn our attention to the different chemicals generated within the body that regulate the way we function, both physically and mentally. Some of these are hormones, which are produced in the endocrine glands and released into the bloodstream. Others are neurotransmitters, which are produced in nerve cells, primarily in the brain, and passed on through the nervous system from nerve cell to nerve cell. Some of these chemicals can act as both hormones and neurotransmitters and have different functions in each of these forms.

The following eight hormones and neurotransmitters are among the most significant:

1. **Endocannabinoids** regulate pain, mood, appetite and sleep.
2. **Dopamine** gives the feeling of reward and victory, but can be associated with addiction as behaviours such as gambling, taking drugs and eating fast food can boost our dopamine levels.
3. **Adrenaline** contributes to the fight-or-flight stress response by increasing heart rate and blood flow to muscles.
4. **Endorphins** relieve pain and stress and boost mood. They are released in response to pleasurable activities.
5. **Cortisol** regulates inflammation, blood pressure, blood sugar and sleep. Your body increases cortisol production at times of stress to give you an energy boost to deal with the stressful situation, but if you are constantly stressed and cortisol levels remain high this can lead to disorders such as anxiety, depression, heart disease and difficulty sleeping.
6. **Serotonin** regulates mood, digestion, libido and sleep. Low serotonin levels can lead to problems in these areas.
7. **Monoamine oxidase (MAO)** destroys the mood-boosting neurotransmitters serotonin and dopamine. Therefore, some anti-depressant medications operate by inhibiting the effect of MAO.
8. **Gamma-aminobutyric acid (GABA)** slows down the brain and calms the mind.

It is not important to know everything there is to know about all these chemicals, but just from this brief summary it is clear that there is an important link between what happens in our bodies and what happens in our minds. The *bushi* warriors of the past would not have been aware of substances such as serotonin, cortisol and the rest, but they did recognize the mind–body connection. This is evident from the Japanese word for "mind", which is *shin* or *kokoro* (心). *Shin* is often translated as "heart-mind"; it means your inner self, your identity, the emotions that you hold inside. Remember, consciousness and human awareness are found in the dual dialogue in your thoughts. For the Japanese, this conversation exists within *shin*, the heart-mind; the brain is just the physical matter which holds it.

The Japanese character for *shin* (心) is also the foundation character for *nin* (忍), which means "endurance". This in turn is the foundation for the character *kannin* (堪忍), which means "forbearance". All of these characters start with the heart. *Nin* (忍) is also the base character used to represent the famous ninja (忍者), who were historically known as *shinobi no mono*.

**The chemical processes that occur within your body have identifiable effects on the mind. Following the paths of Zen and swordsmanship will not enable you to override these natural activities, but by instilling correct reactions and thoughts you will be able to make the mind–body connection work for you and not against you.**

## Lesson 53. Train your inner-mind

The mind is a mysterious place, the workings of which are beyond words. However, words are all we have to describe the little that we do know, or think we know, about the mind. Three words in particular – conscious, subconscious and unconscious – are used in Western psychology to refer to the main aspects of the mind and consciousness. Defining and distinguishing between these aspects is not simple, but Sigmund Freud used an iceberg as a metaphor to help us understand. According to this metaphor, any ice above the water represents the conscious mind. If you peer down into the water, with some effort you can make out the subconscious mind. However, you can only see a little way into the water. Beyond that, it gets too dark to see anything; this is the realm of the unconscious mind.

The thoughts you are aware of come from the conscious mind, and thoughts that are not directly relevant to what you are consciously thinking about but "pop" into your mind come from the subconscious mind. In contrast, the unconscious mind deals with things that happen automatically without any thoughts, conscious or subconscious, being involved at all. Consider the difference between suppression and repression: if you suppress a thought, you make a conscious effort to stop thinking that thought; whereas a repressed thought – for example, a memory of a traumatic experience – is one that has been unconsciously blocked from entering your awareness.

It can help to look more closely at the words "subconscious" and "unconscious". The prefix "sub" means "below", so subconscious means "below conscious"; while "un" means "not", so unconscious means "not conscious", i.e. "not awake". However, the situation is not helped by the fact that in psychology the two terms are often used interchangeably. Therefore, I will generally use the term "inner-mind" to refer to the mind that makes decisions for you.

The inner-mind (which is also called adaptive unconscious) is the part of the brain that makes you leap back before you get hit by a car, or swerve your own car out of the way if someone steps in front of it. It is what makes you instinctively catch a ball that you did not know was being thrown or swat a fly before it hits the corner of your eye. All of this is said to happen in the cerebellum (see lesson 40). The ways in which the cerebellum helps you in emergency situations are as follows:

1. Maintaining equilibrium
2. Running an internal clock
3. Acting as an internal gyroscope
4. Regulating rhythm in movement
5. Synchronizing head and eye movements
6. Calculating the speed and trajectory of outside objects
7. Measuring the body's position in time and space
8. Coordinating muscle movements and reactions
9. Balancing the eyes when the body is moving (known as the vestibulo-ocular reflex)
10. Engaging the body's intuition.

These are the key functions that you are looking to access. The brain already has the capability to do everything you need it to do; you just have to guide it to do its job in the activity that you are practising. Although swords did not exist when the cerebellum developed in the human brain, you can "teach" this part of your brain to make your body react in a way that is best for sword combat. This you do through proper and continuous training.

**Train your inner-mind to make necessary actions automatically through muscle memory. Every athlete, racing car driver, fighter pilot and stage magician does this. What do they have in common? Dedication and practice.**

## Lesson 54. Explore the world with the six senses and six conscious states

In the Asian tradition there are six sense organs and six conscious states.

The six sense organs are:

1. Eyes
2. Ears
3. Nose
4. Tongue
5. Body
6. Mind.

The six conscious states, which are functions of the six sense organs, are:

1. Sight
2. Hearing
3. Smell
4. Taste
5. Touch
6. Reasoning.

No matter what our situation is, we explore the world through all of the above six sense organs and six sense functions that are available to us. It is through these that we experience desire: to see beautiful things, to listen to what pleases us, to smell and taste what we enjoy and to feel sensory pleasures. It is our mind that attaches to desire, but it is Zen that helps us not to become addicted.

**Do not deny yourself all sensual pleasures. The Buddha himself tried extreme asceticism and found it to be lacking. The middle way is to not have not too much or too little. It is to engage with life's pleasures in a controlled way but never to become addicted to anything.**

## Lesson 55. Heed your sixth sense

"Be it natural phenomena or emergencies in human affairs, these matters can be predicted through *kiki* – sensitivity to *chi*. Those who are experienced in military affairs show acute discernment in this matter, but it is not a level normal people can reach."

*The Book of Samurai*

The term "sixth sense", a heightened perception beyond the physical senses, is based on the Western model of five senses: sight, hearing, smell, taste and touch. As we have just learned, the Eastern system has six senses. However, we will continue to use the term "sixth sense", because it is so well established in Western culture.

The sixth sense, also known as extra-sensory perception (ESP), has not been scientifically proven to exist, but we have all experienced situations where we have made decisions based not on any rational, observable evidence but on intuition, or "gut feeling". This is similar to a phenomenon known as thin slicing (see lesson 79).

One story holds that the samurai Yagyu Munenori was sitting contemplating cherry blossoms when he suddenly felt danger.

However, there was no danger: the only person anywhere near was his loyal attendant, who was standing behind him. Annoyed at himself for his over-sensitivity, Munenori explained to his servant what had just happened. His servant confessed that at the very moment Munenori had sensed danger the servant was idly wondering whether he could cut the master swordsman down from behind. Thus, Munenori was relieved to discover that his sixth sense was still in working order.

The *yamabushi*, translated as "those who prostrate themselves in the mountains", is a group of Japanese Buddhist hermit monks whose main aim is to push their endurance until they reach an extreme state of realization and "magical" extra-sensory power. Ignoring the fact that the Buddha taught the avoidance of extremes, is it possible that these monks can build up their intuition to such an intense level? Whatever the answer to this question, the goal of a heightened sense of awareness, where the mind is clear of delusion and can quickly identify threats and sense when something is out of place, would clearly be desirable to achieve. It is up to you if you believe that this is possible and, if so, whether it is achievable by mystical or by practical means.

**Trust your gut feeling. Scientific discovery may be one of the foundations of human progress, but some things run deeper than logical, observable experience. Exploring the esoteric is part of your journey; just do not become bogged down in dogma during that quest. An open mind is a receptive mind.**

## Lesson 56. Conquer delusion

The Zen monk Takuan states that delusion is ignorance; it is not to see the world as it actually is but instead to imprint your own view upon it. Remember that Buddha-mind or Buddha-nature is your true state, which is eternal yet covered by layers of debris, and that your task is to clean the mind to reveal the correct state below. Unless you do this and do it daily, you are living in delusion. When you make errors of perception such as taking what people say out of context, getting angry at perceived insults and prejudging people, you are living in delusion.

It could be argued that delusion is a fundamental aspect of human nature, that our minds are innately unclear. This is akin to the Christian concept of original sin, the idea that we have all been tainted by Adam's succumbing to temptation. Divinity exists within us all, but delusion distorts our perception of reality. It is your own thoughts that are the problem, not what others think, feel or say. Through meditation and correct contemplation, your mind will become clear of delusion. However, if you continue down the wrong path, it will twist your mind in knots and take you ever further away from the Great Realization. Delusion is the greatest of enemies.

**Be brutally honest with yourself. Make it a point to identify the negative aspects of your personality and tackle them. Consider not what appears to be best for you in the short term, but what is fundamentally correct within the situation. Every time you do this you remove a layer of the delusion that is obscuring your view of reality.**

## Lesson 57. Discover the secret of *mu*

This is quite a deep secret, so pay attention. The Chinese and Japanese character *mu* (無) means "absence"; in contrast, the character *u* (有) means "presence". *Mu* is an important concept in Zen, to be found at the root of key terms such as: *mushin* (無心), "no-mind"; *mukei* (無形), "no-shape"; *mujutsu* (無術), "no-skill"; and *muho* (無法), "no-principles". However, be careful not to misunderstand these ideas based on their common English translations. For example, *mushin* ("no-mind") does not mean that someone has no mind, nor does it connote absent-mindedness. *Mushin* would be better translated as one of the following: "the absence of consciousness", i.e. to be in a state of unconscious reaction; "the absence of an observable mind"; or "the absence of restricted thinking".

Meanings can subtly change depending on the situation. In a good translation, a word or term may be translated differently in different contexts to reflect these subtle changes of meaning. I would argue that it is misleading to translate *mu* as "no" or "without", because, although *mu* is indeed the absence of something, that absence is temporary; the "something" that is absent will manifest itself at some point. The apple of an apple tree may not be there in winter and spring, but it will manifest itself by summer and autumn. The apple changes state from *mu* ("absence") to *u* ("presence"), but it always exists – either as a potential apple or an actual apple. It is important to understand *mu* and *u* as an opposing but complementary pair of states.

Similarly, the inner-mind is there always, but it is hidden from sight. Your goal is to detach from conscious thought and allow the inner-mind to take over your body and act for you. The inner-mind comes from a state of hiding into a state of control. This is what the ancient Zen and sword masters were trying to achieve. Engaging in intense sports, driving home without remembering, forgetting yourself in a moment of ecstasy or total focus on a single action, these are examples of the real *mushin* – the absence of the conscious mind. This is far more difficult to achieve in Zen then it is in swordsmanship. In a dangerous situation like a sword fight, the inner-mind will push your conscious mind out of the driver's seat and take over; while in the unthreatening context of Zen meditation you are trying to coax the inner-mind out of its natural habitat, the deep warmth at the bottom of your brain, so that it can take a leading role – something it does not really want to do. *Mushin* in meditation is therefore much harder to achieve. It is not sleep, it is not empty-mindedness, it is not focused concentration on not thinking – it is a free-flowing mind which floats and does not pay heed to any thoughts that gather. It is a state of detachment and bliss.

Now let us look at some other examples of *mu* in action. *Mukei* (無形) is translated as "formlessness", but this does not mean to have no form in the sense of being without ability or training or cohesion. It is about being so well trained that you do not need to take up basic forms. What do we mean by form, though? All sportspeople at first adopt the correct stances and techniques for their sport; painters sketch out angles, light sources and shadows; soldiers gather into formations and move in unison. However, the most skilled practitioners are able to transcend this idea of form. This is similar to the concept of *shuhari*, which we discussed in lesson 44. When an expert does something within their expertise, it looks simple. This is an example of *mukei*, the absence of form, because you see only the end results, not the hard forms that have gone into such apparently effortless movement. Think of an ice skater or a ballet dancer and the work it takes to look so graceful. Imagine doing this with swordsmanship.

People also often refer to the confusing idea of "form within no-form", another cliché left over from outdated orientalism. Form within no-form means to look casual and inattentive but to be able to strike out and gain victory because you have an excellent command of all the basics and do not rely more heavily on some techniques than on others. This is just a way of saying that someone is fluid in their skill and expert in adjusting to the situation. Somehow, they always pick the correct thing to do. A tennis player in a fast rally is an example of both formlessness and of form within no-form. If you take a snapshot of them in play their form would be perfect, but when you run the video it seems like they just move around the court at random and keep happening to be in the right place at the right time. Football players appear to all run about in different directions, to have no uniformity, yet they are all keeping the overall team shape in mind. Like an army, they are in formation but acting independently, which to an untrained eye seems like chaos. In the ancient world, the war general whose soldiers appeared to be slovenly, but who could, upon a signal, switch his army into a fierce fighting monster capable of swift and decisive action, was a master of form within no-form.

This is the secret of *mu*: it is not really an absence, it is the presence of something deeper, better trained and more in control. It is your inner-mind at work.

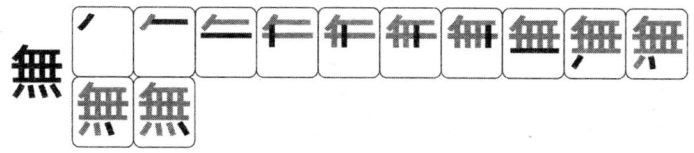

The character for *mu* (無) represents "nothingness" but also "absence". Used in combination with other characters, it can sometimes convey the idea of "potential".

**Excellence is free-flowing movement between the basics of your craft. People look for deep secrets and magical ways to become great at something, but greatness is built on complete command of fundamental skills. *This* is the secret you are looking for. Practise, practise, practise what you do and mastery will come.**

## Lesson 58. Pass through the Gateless Gate

"A good *shinobi* can take in other people's minds without letting them know. He can pass through the Gateless Gate without being recognized, which is indeed a terrifying skill."

*True Path of the Ninja*

The Gateless Gate, known in Japanese as *mumonkan* (無門関), is another concept based on the character of *mu* (無) which we investigated in the previous lesson. In your training in either Zen or swordsmanship you may have heard of this idea. (It is also the title of a famous collection of Zen koans, so do not get confused in your research.)

At first glance, the term Gateless Gate appears to be a paradox. How can a gate be without a gate? However, it is better understood as a mental obstacle rather than a physical barrier. Directly translated, it reads as, "while there is no gate, there is a barrier." The real meaning is that your own mind contains a puzzle that you have to solve, or escape from. A spiritual block is what stops you gaining enlightenment, but this blockage is only in your mind. You are trapped behind a barrier that will not open. You have the key to this barrier, but you do not know where the keyhole is.

Another way of looking at this concept is to imagine that you are walking down a long road. At the end of the road is realization, which is symbolized by a great light. You cannot see the source of the light but you can see its glow, so you know it is there. This is the road to *nirvana*. Along the road are seemingly impenetrable gateways, which are stopping you from reaching the light and warmth at the end. However, you can pass through each of these by looking inside your mind and killing any negativity, such as prejudice, greed, hatred and selfishness, thinking no evil, speaking no evil, doing no evil, and focusing only on your own journey. If you can do all this, the barriers will melt away and you will be able to walk on to the next spiritual checkpoint – but if you cannot do this, the gateway will remain closed and you will be stuck behind it or, worse, you may wander off the road and go in the wrong direction entirely.

**If you are stuck or frustrated, it may be that your life has become too complex. Go back to basics: clean up your diet and your friendships, tidy up your mind and your environment. Read something simple and profound. Breathe, meditate, focus, relax. This kind of reset always works.**

## Lesson 59. Cultivate the unaffected mind

Like *mushin* (see lesson 57), *fudoshin* (不動心) is a term that is commonly translated in a misleading way. You will often see it rendered as "the immovable mind", but *fudoshin* is not immovable nor is it stubborn; it is *unaffected*. Think of a statue in a garden. Birds may perch on it, bees buzz around it, sun shine on it or snow fall on it, but none of these will change the statue's natural state. The most beautiful or ugly events may happen before the statue – the performance of a Shakespearean play or the creation of an exquisite painting, a brutal assault or a viper sinking its venom into a defenceless child – but no matter what happens, nothing will change the statue; it remains resolute. Likewise, when the moon hangs above a stormy ocean, no matter how much the ocean rages, the moon is not affected.

The reason for translating *fudoshin* as "the unaffected mind" rather than "the immovable mind" is that you can and should decide to change your thoughts and you should remain flexible. The key to the concept of *fudoshin* is that nothing external should change your mind for you. The moon moves across the sky, the statue can be shifted to a different location; they are not immovable, but they remain unaffected. Similarly, you can change your own mental state, but no one can change it for you.

The difference between *fudoshin* ("the unaffected mind") and *mushin* ("the absence of conscious thoughts") is that with *fudoshin* you are not allowing anything outside of you to alter your mental state, whereas *mushin* is a temporary state of free flow during which the conscious mind is not active. If you are in a state of *mushin*, an external factor can interrupt your flow; but when you have *fudoshin* as well, nothing can affect your free-flowing state and everything you do comes naturally.

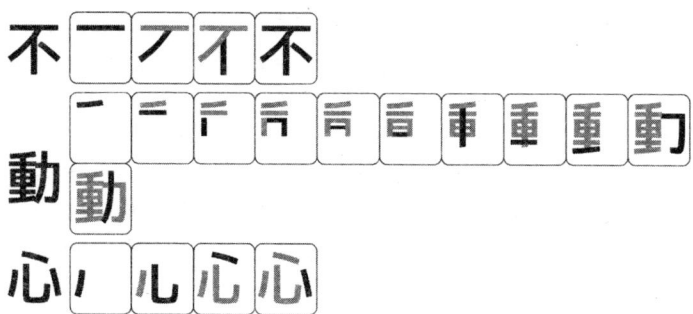

The Chinese characters for *fudoshin* (不動心) literally mean "no-movement-mind", but context tells us that it is things outside your mind that try to move you.

**Train your mind to not be affected by external influences. Once you let someone or something change your attitude**

then you will be put on the back foot. You will fail at this often, like many of the lessons in this book, but when you notice that you have failed, imagine yourself as the unaffected statue or moon and try again.

## Lesson 60. Overcome the stopping mind

"For close combat or sword fighting, there is no way to describe how to do such things at length. Therefore, just be sure to always train yourself with swordsmanship, sword-drawing and other such subjects. Tactics always depend on the time and place."

*The Book of Ninja*

We have spoken about inner-mind and conscious mind, but let us now introduce the terms "implicit memory" and "explicit memory", both of which are long-term memory functions. Try to describe how to ride a bike or catch a ball. Specify every angle change and weight shift, every elevation, rotation and movement of the arms and legs, and so on. It is maybe not impossible to describe all this, but it is absolutely unnecessary. We just learn how to do such things without ever thinking about them. This is implicit memory. In contrast, explicit memory requires deliberate effort from the conscious mind. It is what we use to remember past events, the ingredients to a recipe, the lyrics to a song, a chronological list of the kings and queens of England, and so on.

In situations that require a free-flowing state, explicit memory is not helpful. However, under pressure, sometimes we try to impose logic on our actions, consciously weighing up what is best to do when normally we would let our inner-mind take over. This is what the Japanese grandmasters termed "stopping". Too much thinking leads to faltering. It is like the well-known saying in sports "paralysis through analysis". When an athlete focuses on remembering the minor details of their training and gets caught up in thinking about what is happening instead of just responding naturally, they stumble in the heat of action.

The Zen priest Takuan also discusses the abiding mind, or the fixed mind, the mind that stops in one place. Reading a book, peeling an apple, driving a car are normally done in the free-flowing state of *mushin*. However, if the mind stops and suddenly focuses on what you are doing, you may mentally hesitate: skip a sentence by mistake, cut your finger, miss a gear, take the wrong turn and so on. These are all examples of stopping. It is the jarring change from a free-flowing state to a consciously active one where you are trying to make decisions but your mind cannot keep pace with the situation.

In swordsmanship and Zen, if you focus on the cut you are making or on the meditation you are performing, your mind has stopped. It is no longer free-flowing and reactive. In swordsmanship, it is wrong to think about what your opponent will do next. Likewise, in meditation, when your mind drifts, it drifts to something else. It stops at whatever you are thinking about. The lesson here is that it is wrong to have a mind that micromanages your actions or that thinks of something beyond the situation you are in.

The ideal state to be in is one of *mu* emptiness where the inner-mind takes control. Do not think of here and now or there and then. Pop your thoughts like balloons and act, react or wait. Imagine that you are playing table tennis, a sport where there is no time to stop the flow. The action is so fast that the moment you make a move, another move is required. If you stop to think about where the last shot landed or analyse the positioning of the other player, you will soon lose. Swordsmanship is the same: attack, defend, move, repost, parry – there is no time for the mind to stop on anything. If it does, even just once, it will be game, set and match, but this time for life.

**There are times when it is good to sit and think, daydream, consciously analyse a problem or a subject, but there are also times when you should let go and allow the years of hard training to pay off, trust your body and inner-mind to know what they are doing. Make sure you know when to think and when to let go.**

# Lesson 61. Polish the mirror

If you put paper, cloth or even iron into the ground they will degrade. Paper will quickly become pulpy and tear; cloth will take longer to break down, but the result will be the same; over time, iron will rust. However, diamonds and other gems, though covered in mud, will remain brilliant underneath.

The mind has been likened to a jewel. No matter how many layers of impurity cover it, its essence remains the same and it can be cleaned and returned to its original state. This represents your true inner potential. The mirror is another common metaphor for the mind in Japanese culture and Shinto shrines often have a mirror as their sacred object. A mirror may become covered in dust, but the dust can be polished away to gain a clear reflection.

Of course, the process of cleaning and polishing becomes harder the longer we leave the dirt to build up. This is why polishing the mind should be something we do regularly. If you polish your mind each day by practising Zen, your view of the world will be clear and unclouded and that is the way you should live your life.

**We often misread how things really are, misinterpret what people say and look for negative meanings that may not be there. If we clean our mind each day and return it to a polished state, we can see how the world really is, be it negative or positive. Then with a proper understanding we can react to it accordingly.**

# Lesson 62. Calm the ocean of emotion

The Japanese also use the idea of the moon reflected in water to represent the mind. Try taking the lid off a jar of water under moonlight. The moon's reflection will appear instantly upon the surface of the water even on such a small scale. Wherever there is water and moonlight, the reflection will appear just like that. Look in a thousand puddles and you will find that each one has its own moon reflected in it.

It is the same for the moon over a sea at night. The moon and the water exist individually and the reflection is a measure of how well they are aligned. If the waves are choppy, the reflection of the moon is disturbed; if it is dead calm, then the reflection is much clearer. This is a representation of the mind and how it reflects the external world. Calm water "sees" the world perfectly, while turbulent water distorts the alignment. The water is your mind, the moon is the reality outside of you. Zen calms the water and makes the world's reflection clear.

This is all about emotion. Be it love, anger, hate, fear or sadness, emotion disrupts mental clarity. There is an "ocean of emotion" within you and your job is to follow the path of the Zen warrior to calm the waves.

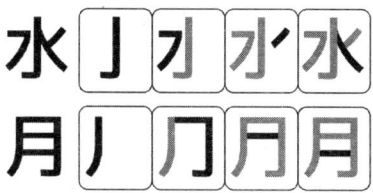

The Japanese term *suigetsu* (水月) contains the Chinese characters for "water" and "moon".

**Your mind is not always settled and your reactions may well be incorrect. Use meditation or a period of introspection each day to help calm your mind so that your view of external reality does not become distorted.**

## Lesson 63. Penetrate the minds of others

"Because your mind is working properly it allows you to fulfil your purpose and shows what is called *shinmyoken*."

### *True Path of the Ninja*

*Shinmyoken* (心妙劍) is the term used by the *bushi* to describe the concept of penetrating the minds of others. It can be translated as "the mind which penetrates into the mysteries of the human heart", or as "the sword which cuts through the obscurity of the mind". It is both to cut through the intentions of the enemy and to understand the delusions of your own mind. If you split an apple tree in half, where are the apples? If you cut open a chicken, where are the eggs? Future apples or eggs cannot be seen within the tree or chicken that will bear them. They exist in *mu* (無), "potential", as described in lesson 57. Likewise, if you "split open" your opponent you cannot see the thoughts in their mind; you cannot see what actions they are planning to take. But by observing this person closely and with a clear mind, looking at how they have acted in the past and identifying patterns in their behaviour, you can accurately predict their future actions in any given situation. This is how you use *shinmyoken*, "the penetrating mind". Check your opponent's behaviour, check the calmness of your own mind, and then try to intuit their actions.

There are various ways to construct the term *shinmyoken*. The most common uses the characters for "heart" (心), "mysterious" (妙) and "sword" (剣). Note that the last of these characters is the general ideogram for "sword" (剣), not the specific one for the Japanese *katana* (刀).

**Take note of other people's behaviour, but always rigorously check that how you perceive them is not a distortion of your own mind.**

## Lesson 64. Be like stone

An egg has a hard shell to protect its soft internals, but if you exert too much pressure on it the structure collapses. This is the same with people. We all have an outer shell, the persona that we project to the world. Some people may give the impression of being tough and resilient, but when they are put under even a small amount of external pressure they crack. If a situation "heats up" they become addled and confused, emotional and distracted. In contrast, a stone pebble can be heated to high temperatures, thrown at walls, kicked about, hit with a stick, dropped off a cliff, yet it remains unchanged. Even if the pressure is so great that it does crack, its internal structure will not fundamentally change.

Therefore, the goal of a Zen warrior is to become like a solid, rock-hard stone egg and not only maintain a tough exterior but also develop internal strength. When people have full mastery over their mind, they can face the prospect of adversity and even death without any change in their emotional state. This is my teaching of the stone egg and is the only lesson here that has not come from historical research.

**Keep an egg-shaped stone on your altar or on display somewhere sacred to you. Remind yourself each day that you have to become like this stone, unmoved and unchanged by external pressure. We all fail at this, but the stone can symbolize your journey toward greater resistance.**

## Lesson 65. Let your mind flow freely

We have spoken of the mind many times, but now we will focus on the free-flowing mind. This is the state of mind you achieve when you are fully engaged in what you are doing in that moment, but are able to flow freely from one situation to the next as required. You move from moment to moment, keeping in the now.

Let us say, for example, that you are reading a book. The free-flowing mind focuses fully on the words on the page you are reading, savouring each one. It does not jump ahead to thinking about what you will be doing next or speculating how the book will end. It enjoys what you are doing and does not look beyond the moment.

However, if your circumstances change drastically, the free-flowing mind will allow you to move immediately to this new situation without hesitating. For example, if, while you are reading your book, water spills on you, you seldom carry on reading – instead, you react immediately. This is the same for a swordsman.

The perfect free-flowing mind that the ancient masters talked about is like a ball on the ocean which floats with the waves. It is your task to be unaffected and respond to every move in the most effective way. However, the move from one situation to the next will always start with a conscious thought before the inner-mind takes over. For example, at the beginning of a sword fight, a swordsman may think: "The enemy is in a high guard, I will move lower"; or "Is there something behind me, or something behind the enemy?", and so on. But the moment the action starts there should be no thoughts, just reactions. The logical brain does nothing at this point and you have to rely on your training. You never rise to the occasion; you drop to your current level of training. Always remember this.

**Never let your mind wander when you are engaged in an activity. Use your logical mind to make decisions while there is time and then let go when the action starts.**

## Lesson 66. Remember death

"If you cannot detach yourself from death, then you will fear everything. It is said that nothing is a greater change than your own death, think on this. This is the same as to stop breathing through a fear of ageing."

*The Book of Samurai*

All humans have to face the prospect of death, but warriors are closer to it. Remember that Buddhism tells us we are stuck inside the cycle of life and death and are tied to reincarnation, which also places us in a loop of karmic consequence, be it negative or positive. A *bushi* reconciles himself to death by aiming to lead a fulfilling life in the meantime, and this is a good attitude for us all.

Western culture is also full of reminders of our mortality. In art, symbols such as skulls, coffins and hourglasses are often depicted. These are known as *memento mori* – the Latin for "remember death" – and they signify the inevitability of death. The Danse Macabre, a common representation of skeletons dancing with humans, is another visual statement of this universal truth. It tells us that no matter who you are, death will find you. Similarly, the vast charnel houses filled with bones remind us of our fate. None of this is morbid, nor are the *bushi* morbidly attracted to death. It is all part of the acceptance of the cyclical nature of life. Whether a person believes that they are going to be reincarnated after death, or that they will go to Heaven or Hell, or even that they will cease to exist, everyone is captured inside of life in this moment and knows that they will one day die.

As a Zen warrior, your task is to come to terms with your mortality and follow a pathway that will eventually take you out of the cycle of life and death. This goal is not an easy one and your attitude to death will fluctuate: on some days you will dread death; other days you will welcome it. The challenge is to flatten out these variations and remain stable in your own mind, no matter what is happening around you.

**Keep your own *memento mori*. Use it to remember that the clock is ticking and the hourglass is draining. Life should be fun, but the more you just exist without clear purpose, the more lifetimes you will have to serve. The universe is waiting for you to do the work. No one can do it for you.**

## Lesson 67. Follow the Ten Ox-Herding Pictures

Connected to Zen are the famous Ten Ox-Herding Pictures. Sometimes you will see these referred to as the Ten Bull Pictures. Both are acceptable translations. This illustrated scroll takes the reader on a ten-stage journey from total ignorance all the way through to full awakening, just like the journey that the Buddha made.

The ten steps to attaining Buddhahood illustrated by the ten pictures are:

1. The search for spiritual truth begins.
2. Catching a glimpse of spiritual truth, you see the possibility of enlightenment.
3. Follow the path which leads to spiritual truth and find the correct direction.
4. It will become difficult to continue on the correct way. Past ways can be a distraction or a hindrance, so you really have to focus on the path.
5. You may have some control over your progress and now you can distinguish between various aspects of the mysterious.
6. At this stage, you have control of your mind and can progress with ease.
7. Having achieved high ability, do not slacken in your dedication to the search for wisdom.
8. Emptiness is obtained by stripping away the idea of self. Now you will start to see the world as it truly is.
9. At this stage, pure clarity is obtained and reality is known to you.
10. You can now return to society as a sage and as a spiritual being.

These ten stages apply to all people seeking enlightenment, whether it be in the way of the sword or any other way. No Zen warrior should be without the Ten Ox-Herding Pictures, so it is best that you frame a copy and put it on your wall or make your own scroll.

**Spiritual awakening can happen at any time but it takes work. Realistically, you will have to work for many lifetimes to achieve enlightenment, so make sure you have a spiritual map like the Ten Ox-Herding Pictures to help you plan your route and track your progress.**

## Lesson 68. Understand Buddhahood and bodhisattvas

When investigating Buddhism in general and Zen in particular, you will come across the terms Buddhahood and bodhisattva. These need some explanation – particularly bodhisattva, as this term has a range of meanings.

A person who has reached Buddhahood has attained total understanding. They have passed through the last of the Gateless Gates (see lesson 58); they have had an indescribable realization which allows them to live in a state of complete bliss known as *nirvana*. When they die, universal law will pull them out of *samsara* – the cycle of birth, death and rebirth – and they will finally be extinguished from reality, which is a positive thing. Whether they cease to exist at this point or whether they enter a different form of reality cannot be known.

The term bodhisattva is sometimes used to refer to the Buddha in his life before he became fully enlightened, but it more commonly denotes a person who has decided that they want to become a buddha; this is not a fleeting wish but a dedicated spiritual commitment supported by a living buddha. (Note the difference between "the Buddha", which refers to Siddhartha Gautama, the original man whose discoveries and teachings gave rise to Buddhism, and "a buddha", someone who has followed the Buddha's path to *nirvana*.) Therefore, a bodhisattva can be thought of as a pre-buddha. Bodhisattvas range from those who have just set out on their path to heroic super-beings who are imbued with supernatural powers. At the highest level, a bodhisattva can be someone who has become enlightened but decided to postpone their entry into *nirvana* in order to help other people achieve their own spiritual awakening.

**Dedicate yourself to the spiritual path, but only do this if you are ready. Be honest with yourself about how far you have travelled along the spiritual way. Make a concerted effort to work harder than you did in the last incarnation and promise to work even harder in the next.**

## Round-up

In part three we touched upon the basics of brain chemistry and established what the inner-mind is. We discussed the Eastern conception of the physical senses and explored the idea of the "sixth sense", an extra-sensory intuition. We learned how to overcome delusion, avoid the trap of the stopping mind, and penetrate our opponent's mind. We also discovered how to pass through the Gateless Gate, use the secrets of *mu* and *fudoshin*, polish your mirror-mind and calm the waters of your emotions. We explored meditation in greater depth and outlined the path to enlightenment through Zen's famous Ten Ox-Herding Pictures. The next step in our journey is to consider how we engage the enemy.

# PART 4.
# ENGAGE THE ENEMY

Having focused primarily on our relationship with our own mind and emotions and with the universe, now we will turn our attention to the various ways in which we interact with an enemy or opponent. The famous Chinese military strategist Sun Tzu said that to defeat an enemy you must do so before they even realize that there is any prospect of conflict. To be in a better position before you engage with the enemy, you must disguise your own rhythms to create confusion. In this section, we will study how to observe the enemy, set your range and get the balance right between strategy and intuition. We will discuss the question of whether to make the first strike, or even if you should strike at all. There are also the subtle arts of receiving an attack and finding the balance point within a conflict. We will look at reaction and rationalize the mystery of the Japanese *kiai*, or energy shout. A battle or contest typically ends with one side winning and the other losing. Therefore, we will discover what to do if you are victorious and what to do if you are defeated, and to know the difference between the sword of life and the sword of death. We will also continue our journey into the subject of death by investigating how to contemplate our mortality without it becoming a morbid fascination. Finally, we will look at the compassion you need to move along the Zen path and assess just how close to becoming a buddha you really are.

## Lesson 69. Defeat the enemy before the war

"Now the general who wins a battle makes many calculations in his temple ere the battle is fought. The general who loses a battle makes but few calculations beforehand."

**Sun Tzu (6th or 5th century BC)**

Sun Tzu tells us to set up any conflict so that we will win with the minimum of effort. If it is done correctly, warfare is 99 per cent preamble and 1 per cent strike. However, even the best-planned campaign will be costly, in terms of both lives lost and resources spent. Therefore, it is better to avert the war before it happens, as we trust our politicians to do.

Zen would have it that we should also identify our own internal tensions and resolve them before they break out into conflict. Identify both enemies without and enemies within before harmony is disturbed. As trouble either around you or within your own mind starts to gather, make moves to eradicate it. Search and destroy any negative thoughts and nip any external threats in the bud before they arise. Be watchful in all aspects of your life, including social relationships, so that you can gain victory in a single strike. Overall, keep one eye on the distance to try to identify future conflict before it gains momentum and stay alert with regard to your immediate surroundings.

**Be an island unto yourself with small connecting bridges to others, but make ready to block any attack that comes. Try your best never to burn your bridges, as it is harder to rekindle a friendship once the connection has been broken, but also make sure you are not left open to attack.**

## Lesson 70. Learn to perform under pressure

We all know that to win you should be "in the zone". From *Star Wars* to *The Last Samurai*, Hollywood films have told us to "let go" and "be at one" with the situation, and they are not wrong. The whole point of Zen is to detach from the logical mind and engage that part of the brain you have no control over but which has control over you. Yet even for the *bushi* this was a difficult thing to do.

The Yagyu clan swordsmen taught the following six ways to maintain a proper mindset even in the most pressurized situation:

1. Totally eradicate the idea of winning or losing.
2. Do not get bogged down in technicalities.
3. Do not immediately rush to display all understanding and knowledge.
4. Do not resort to intimidating or overawing your opponent.
5. Do not allow your opponent to intimidate or overawe you.
6. Do not focus on the above five points during action.

The same lesson appears time and time again in samurai literature. Do not focus on the logical mind, do not focus on trying not to focus; instead train hard and then let go of all that training and trust yourself. Avoid your mind stopping at any point and just be. It is one of the most difficult things in the world to do when the pressure on you is immense, but remember that this is what you are training for.

**Avoid focusing on the concept of focus. Once you start to think "I must focus on this" or "I must not focus on that", you end up focusing on something and not letting your body act.**

## Lesson 71. Know how to observe the enemy

"In a fight with a great sword, those who can discern the direction of the opponent's sword can understand his gaps and will win, while those who cannot see this will lose."

*The Book of Ninja*

"Always look the enemy in the eye" goes the stereotype. However, a real *bushi* would tell you something quite different. Sword manuals such as the Gorin no Sho by Miyamoto Musashi, the Heiho Kadensho by Yagyu Munenori and Shinkan no Maki by Hagihara Juzo often talk about the various ways of seeing and perception and appear to heavily favour the use of peripheral vision instead of directly looking at the enemy. We have discussed previously just what peripheral vision is (see lesson 39), but let us now discover how it helps in swordsmanship.

Miyamoto Musashi identifies two ways of using the eyes when in combat: the first is *kan no me* (観の目), "observation", which he considered the correct way; the second is *ken no me* (見の目), "seeing", which he considered to be incorrect and "weak". It appears here that Musashi is attempting to describe the difference between peripheral vision (observation) and foveal vision (seeing). Foveal vision is what you use for intense scrutiny of a fixed object. However, too much emphasis on the foveal can detract from the peripheral, which is what you really need in a combat situation, where it is important to pick up on sudden movements across a wide field of vision. It is the difference between trying to swat away a fly and examining it under a microscope.

According to the sword school Yagyu Shinkage Ryu, when you are engaged but are outside of cutting distance, watch the enemy's hands; when you are up close, watch their chest; and when they have the sword held in a high position, watch their elbows. In none of these situations should you look at their face.

The third samurai in our list, Hagihara Juzo, writes about how you should observe your enemy before combat:

"Perception of the mind is speculating about the enemy's mind before you advance upon them. Perception of the eye is to speculate about the enemy's mind by looking at how the enemy's eyes are used. When you master perception of the mind and of the eye, you will automatically be able to achieve perception of the form. Therefore, perception of the form derives from the two points of the mind and of the eye – this is a deep secret ... When you attack the enemy, to consider what the enemy is going to do next is considered as perception of the mind. Perception of the eye and of the form may delay your movement. Therefore, sometimes you should not over-speculate about the enemy. Common people should not try to estimate as mentioned above when fighting."

**The Lost Samurai School**

In summary, never look your opponent in the eye during combat; only do this before combat begins to see if they give anything away about themselves. Instead, look at different parts of their form – their shoulders, their chest, their hands, their elbows – according to the situation. Use peripheral vision to pick up on their movements and then let your unconscious mind make the next move for you.

**If you focus only on what is directly in front of you, you will miss much of what is going on around you. Instead, in all areas of your life, switch between a detailed view and a broad view, and also between immediate and far-reaching factors, so that you cover all aspects.**

## Lesson 72. Move from strategic to intuitive combat

In July and August 2002, the US military staged the Millennium Challenge, an expensive war simulation. The scenario: a rogue military faction in a fictitious Middle Eastern state has seized a group of islands in the Persian Gulf, threatening the safety of international shipping and promoting terrorism in the region. The objective: to neutralize that threat. The participants in the exercise were divided into a blue team (the US forces) and a red team (the rogue faction). Unsurprisingly, the blue team had superior firepower and resources, yet the red team was able to get the better of them, sinking or damaging many of their virtual warships. Why was this the outcome? The red team was led by Paul Van Riper, an experienced general who believed that warfare was a matter of being able to make a series of snap decisions. He went into the exercise with only one plan, a simple one: to discover how many missiles the red fleet could defend against and then fire more than that number from all angles. The blue fleet was "crippled", end of game (although the exercise was suspended and relaunched with rule changes that favoured the blue team).

While a basic strategy is needed, what is more important is the ability to make the right decisions in a short space of time. This ability typically comes from a rich wealth of experience. Gary Klein in his book *Sources of Power* comes to the same conclusion: doctors, nurses, firefighters, emergency responders and so on all have to make important decisions in a time frame that does not allow for the careful deployment of well-thought-out plans. Chess is the same: professional games typically start with a series of rehearsed moves, but later evolve into improvised operations based on countering and outmanoeuvring the opponent. Strategy and plans only serve to start you off at an advantage. For the swordsman, this is also true. Any fixed strategy is outdated the moment the contest begins. Once the decision has been made to move forward into combat, the conscious mind must be abandoned and the inner-mind engaged. This is the difference between strategic planning and intuitive reaction. Both are needed and both rely on professionalism and constant training.

**Make plans for a contest of any kind so that you start at an advantage over an unprepared opponent, and at no disadvantage to a prepared one. However, when the contest starts you should next move into a state of free-flowing reaction where your own sharp mind and training will allow you to choose what move is best in the instant.**

# Lesson 73. Be without observable rhythm

"When your opponent is not going to strike at you with their sword, it is difficult for you to strike at them. Instead, you should strike at the moment that the opponent attacks."

*The Book of Ninja*

Have you heard the conundrum of the fly stopping the train? A train is travelling in one direction while a fly is heading straight for it. According to Newton's laws of motion, an object travelling at speed cannot change direction without stopping first. Thus when the fly hits the train, the fly is both stopped and in contact with a small part of the train, which means that that part of the train must also stop just at the instant when the fly stops to change direction. Thus, a fly can stop a train, even if only for a fraction of a second.

This, of course, is true only in theory, not in observable reality, but what it does illustrate is the *bushi* idea of unobservable rhythm or reacting instantaneously. When you clap your hands, the sound is immediate; when you hit an iron striker on to flint, the spark is immediate; when you look in a mirror, the reflection is also immediate. There is no discernible interval between action and reaction. What we are looking to perform as swordsmen is a single action in two parts but without any apparent interruption between the two. This is *muhyoshi* (無拍子), "the absence of observable rhythm", another concept deriving from the secret of *mu* (無), which we first met in lesson 57. You must have rhythm to fight, but a master's rhythm is unobservable. A competent drummer can hold a predictable, conventional beat, but an expert drummer creates a rhythm all of their own. A decent rhythm guitarist can strum a series of chords over and over, but a top-level player like AC/DC's Malcolm Young could add syncopation to disturb the rhythm while still powering the song forward. There appears to be no gap between what they do with their hands and the perfect result. This holds true for swordsmanship. The perfect interaction flows like liquid. The rhythm is unseen and the fight is finished with no thought, no planning and no breaks in the movement. Within a handful of seconds, the expert swordsman repeatedly finds the right position at the right time.

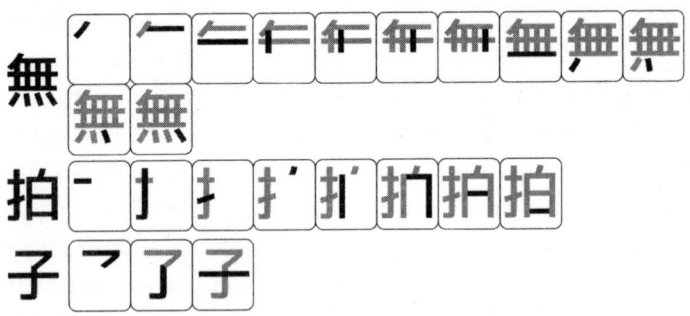

The concept of *muhyoshi* (無拍子) is the foundation for the samurai school known as Muhyoshi Ryu. Sometimes you may see the name given as Mubyoshi Ryu, but the meaning remains the same.

**Get into position immediately and make your move before your opponent has finished making theirs; otherwise, you will be behind.**

## Lesson 74. Set your distance

"On the subject of cutting someone: when they move in to meet you, unless you bring them in close … you will not be able to land your blow with the cutting section of the blade, and if it is not done in this manner then you will only hit with the tip."

*The Book of Samurai*

*Kenmon* (間門) and *maai* (間合い) are terms that relate to Japanese martial arts. *Kenmon* means "gap in the gate", the idea being to find an opening in your opponent's defence. *Maai* means "suitable distance".

Distancing in Japanese swordsmanship is very simple: you can be out of range or you can be within range. Obviously, at some point you have to be in range to hit the enemy, but this of course puts you in their range too. The trick is to come into range at the correct time and to strike without giving your opponent an opportunity to strike back at you. This requires skilful manoeuvring. The samurai Hagihara Juzo states that you should observe the position of your enemy's hands in order to predict and pre-empt the curved path of their sword, before you cross the boundary between safety and danger. This boundary is most often defined as the point at which the swords of the two opponents can cross each other. Once the swords can cross each other, consider yourself in range to make a strike upon the enemy and to be struck by them.

According to the teachings of Natori Masazumi, most people are too far away when they try to strike. This means that they hit with the tip, which does only superficial damage. This was also the case in the Sino-Japanese War of 1937–1945 when Japan invaded China. The Japanese army collected reports after the war on the use of swords (which was still relatively common even in such a modern conflict) and the main finding was that their soldiers were almost always out of range on their first strikes. This may have been because they were more used to practising *kendo*, which employs longer bamboo swords and involves simply tapping your opponent to score a point.

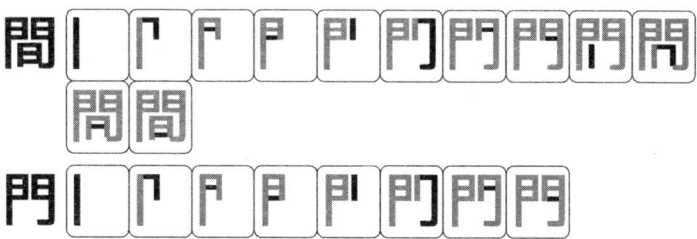

The Chinese characters for the Japanese term *kenmon* (間門), meaning "gap in the gate", are of a gap within a gate (間) and an open gate (門). The idea is to find the gaps in a closed situation.

**Crossing swords is a very dangerous business and there is no way to do it without putting yourself in danger. Up close and personal should be the rule of your training, but always make sure that you are at an advantage when you move in and are able to defend when you move out.**

## Lesson 75. Know when to strike first

Sometimes lords would send samurai on a mission known as *teuchi* (手討), which involved killing a particular person whom the lord wanted dead. This could be an ally or comrade. The officers charged with this duty would often prepare by wearing chainmail, and, when entering the house of their intended victim, would not leave their swords at the front door, as was the custom. The target of an assassination order might pick up on these subtle clues that they were under threat and so make a pre-emptive strike against the officers who had come to kill them.

The lesson here is that, while no one in modern times would advocate the idea of starting a fight, there are times when you must be the initiator. Of course, this does not always entail physical violence, although even in the modern world we all have the right to defend ourselves when we are under threat. The idea of *teuchi* is not redundant in our world, but you should only ever strike first when you have clear evidence that you are about to be attacked.

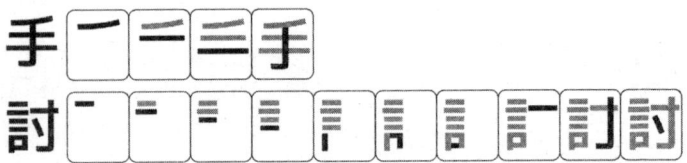

The Japanese term *teuchi* (手討) is made up of the Chinese characters for "hand" (手) and "to strike" (討). Literally, it means "strike with the hand"; in practice, it means to assassinate a target.

**Do not be an aggressor, yet do not be a victim. Always know when action is needed and when it is best to opt for**

diplomacy or retreat. But never forget that sometimes you may have to go on the attack.

## Lesson 76. Know how to receive a strike

"When the enemy attacks you, create distance and capture the enemy timing with your mind. The feeling is like a floating boat on the water which follows the wave or as a bird of the water follows the water itself."

**The Lost Samurai School**

Many martial artists understand the concept of *uke* (受け), which is best translated as "receiving". In modern martial arts, *uketachi* (受け太刀), or "receiving sword", refers to the person who receives a strike, whereas *uchitachi* (打ち太刀), or "striking sword", refers to the person who delivers a strike.

Other examples of referencing the concept of receiving are found in karate. These include *age-uke* (上げ受け), which means "receiving with a lifting motion", and *soto-uke* (外受け), "receiving from the outside", both of which are blocks.

Miyamoto Musashi describes three main ways in which he deals with enemy attacks:

1. *Ukuru koto* (うくる事), "receiving"
2. *Haru koto* (はる事), "slapping"
3. *Ataru koto* (あたる事), "striking".

The secret to countering an enemy strike lies in how you connect with it. Do you blend with the attack? Do you block it by slapping your opponent's blade out of the way? Or do you strike through their attack with a more powerful one of your own? These are your choices and you should practise them thoroughly.

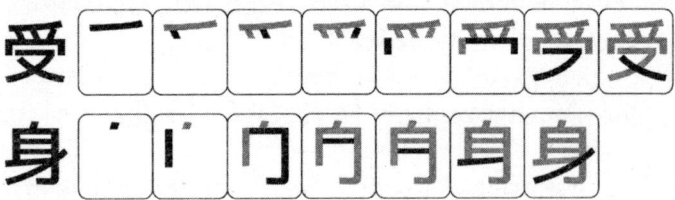

The Japanese term *ukemi* (受身) is made up of the two Chinese characters "receiving" (受) and "body" (身) and is used to refer to the person on the receiving end of a technique being practised.

**Avoid engaging with hostile people if you can. But if you cannot avoid it, choose an appropriate response to their aggression. Absorb their attack and gently try to change their mind. Slap their approach down harshly but follow up with a positive escape. Or stop them in their tracks, blocking their attack.**

## Lesson 77. Find the balance point

The Buddha spoke of the middle way – to neither overindulge nor engage in extreme privation. Finding balance in all things is central to leading a good life.

In Japanese martial arts the concept of *atari* (中り) represents not only balance in the sense of not over-extending yourself but the middle point of a flowing whole. Movements are said to have three stages or beats: the initiation, the middle and the ending. *Atari* is that middle point when everything is floating and pliable.

The term is also used in other contexts to mean the moment of transition between opposing states. Night is dark and day is light, but there is a moment of half-light at dawn and sunset. This is *atari*. Ice is solid and water is liquid, but there is an in-between stage in freezing and thawing that is neither quite solid nor quite liquid. Again, this is *atari*. No matter how wide apart or close together you place the parameters of opposites, there is a moment or space between them.

The idea is to not break down actions into three parts – beginning, middle and end – but to maintain a continuous flow from one part to the next. Just as night becomes day or ice becomes water, there should be no break in your movement. This is similar to the concept of *muhyoshi* (see lesson 73). Even after striking a telling blow, you should still be on the move or following up until you are sure you are safe. There is no dramatic end action stance.

A clear mind, a free-flowing body and no stagnation are fundamental to good health and effective combat.

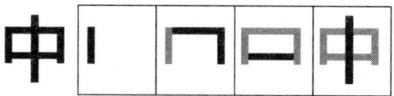

The Chinese character for "the middle" (中) is very important to understanding the Buddha's idea of the middle way.

**Recognize the value of times of transition, those floating, in-between moments. Do not end one thing too abruptly or rush headlong into something new but maintain a steady flow between all phases.**

## Lesson 78. Hone your reactions

Humans can defend themselves instinctively, return a tennis shot, catch a cricket ball or strike out against another person, all without any training at all. Why then do professionals spend their lives training their bodies to perform the same actions over and over again? They do so to train the cerebellum, the unconscious part of the brain, which regulates timing and rhythm and works at the level of thousandths of a second – quicker than your conscious mind could ever compute anything. It coordinates movements, especially actions that have been trained in and practised. It can also judge the speed and trajectory of objects moving through the air. That is why expert tennis players can return balls that are travelling at more than 100 miles an hour.

No matter how complex the movements or the number of variables that need calculating, your cerebellum understands where you are in space and time and coordinates everything around you much faster than the thinking part of your brain can do. Consider the gymnast somersaulting on a narrow beam, the ballet dancer pirouetting, the break dancer vaulting. The more a person trains, the more honed their inner action-clock will become, and the faster and more accurate their reactions will become. The inner-mind has control of all your muscles and tendons within milliseconds of the instructions being transmitted. Just as quickly, our senses send messages back to the inner-mind to give feedback on how accurate or inaccurate the response was, allowing adjustments to be made even in mid-movement.

Where Zen says to use "no-mind", the West says that you should "lose yourself in the action" or "enter the zone". They are one and the same. Do not try to react in time; just let go and let your body do the work it needs to do against your opponent. If you lose, it is not because this teaching is wrong; it is because you have not practised as much or are not as skilled as the person who has defeated you.

**Do not pass up any opportunity to work on your reactions. Take stock of how you react to any situation, be it mental or physical. If you reacted wrongly, adjust your training so that you do better next time.**

## Lesson 79. Trust your intuition

Buddhism teaches us that all things are connected, nothing is permanent, time is a construct and identity is an illusion. However, we are aware of our conscious self and it feels real to us. What we may not be aware of is that we also have another, unconscious self within us, which is controlled by our inner-mind. This means that there are two distinct aspects to our personality, one of which operates at the level of intuition. The inner-mind constantly surveys our environment and processes the information that it detects at phenomenal speed. If it perceives danger, it sends warning signals to your conscious mind. This is your intuition.

In his book *Blink*, Malcolm Gladwell discusses the concepts of "adaptive unconsciousness" and "thin slicing". Adaptive unconsciousness is a term coined by US psychologist Daniel Wegner to describe mental processing such as interpreting information and identifying patterns that is done by the unconscious mind to influence our judgement and decision-making, with the ultimate aim of keeping us safe and well. Developed by psychologists Nalini Ambady and Robert Rosenthal, the theory of thin slicing explains how humans are able to reach accurate judgements based on a very small portion – or, as they would put it, thin slice – of experience.

This is like the French phrase *coup d'oeil* (literally, a "strike made by the eye"), which recognizes our ability to take in a huge amount of information in a single glance. Similarly, birdwatchers use the term "giss" (standing for "general impression of size and shape") to refer to the skill of identifying a bird seen only for an instant.

Gladwell's conclusion is that our inner-mind can select the correct reaction in any situation and identify a problem and calculate a solution to it within an extremely short timeframe. Therefore, we should trust our unconscious survival instinct and follow that "gut feeling" in a dangerous situation. It is only when our conscious mind overrides our intuition that we make mistakes. Once imminent danger has been detected, a person under pressure needs to consciously put themselves – either physically or figuratively – in the best position and then let their inner-mind take over and react in the best way.

**Trust your unconscious mind's early warning system. Your intuition will tell you instantly when something is wrong. It is always better to go with your gut and then work things out later than override it and be sorry.**

## Lesson 80. Harness the energy of shouting

One of the less understood aspects of Japanese martial arts is the *kiai* (気合), the "shout of the spirit". It has come to the West as some ancient magical skill. But is this really the case? There is, in fact, plenty of evidence to suggest that the *kiai* works on a natural rather than a supernatural level. Older studies have shown that grunting and shouting can be effective ways to distract an opponent, whereas more recent ones claim that accompanying a strike with an exclamation can increase the power of the strike by up to 9 per cent. In his book *The Athlete's Way*, Christopher Bergland proposes that grunting is the way in which a practitioner actively dismisses the conscious mind and throws themselves into the realm of unconscious reactions so that muscle memory can take over and provide the best response.

From weightlifting to fencing, shouting is an element found worldwide in physical activities that involve challenge, performance and victory. Warriors in most, if not all, cultures let out a battle cry as a way to elevate their courage and dispel their fear and so there is no need to look at the *kiai* as anything supernatural; it is the Japanese expression of something that is basic to all humans.

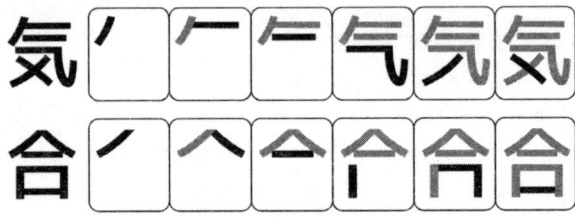

The Chinese characters for *kiai* (気合) are best understood as "the meeting of energy".

**Shouting down your enemy is not the best option; in fact, it is generally the worst. But understand that when it comes to sports or combat, it is sometimes good to tap into the energy of the *kiai*.**

## Lesson 81. Attack when defeated

One of the most famous samurai expressions is to "tighten your helmet cords after a defeat". The meaning is that when you have been defeated, you should move on to the attack without delay. When your enemy has just achieved a victory, they will relax, even if only for a moment, and leave an opening that you can exploit. This can be both literal and metaphorical. For example, if you are struggling with meditation and your mind will not stop chattering, get up, shake it out, sit back down and keep trying until you make some progress. If your new business plan does not work, check all angles and go again. If your team concedes a goal, strike back hard. If you have suffered a fatal wound, get up and fight to the end.

**Defeat is not a permanent condition. Never let a setback actually set you back. Grit your teeth and go again.**

## Lesson 82. Be gracious in victory

The *bushi* most often celebrated a victory by shouting their war cry while holding a severed enemy head in the air. However, modern *kendo* practitioners tend to have a more restrained approach. Older Western traditions would have people be polite in victory; they would normally clap the loser for a valiant effort and shake their hand.

People often bemoan the decline of sportsmanship in the modern world, but this is not a new problem. It is said that when the two great sixteenth-century war leaders Oda Nobunaga and Tokugawa Ieyasu viewed the head of the defeated Takeda Katsuyori, Tokugawa paid the proper respects but Oda was ungracious. Grace in victory and defeat is seen as a positive; sore losers and gloating winners are never appreciated. Note also that there is a practical reason not to get carried away celebrating a victory: you need to be prepared for your defeated opponent to counter-attack.

**It is acceptable to celebrate, but do not rub people up the wrong way by over-celebrating. Always treat your opponents with respect, even when arguing and especially after a victory. Also be aware that you are often most**

vulnerable to a counter-attack when you have just won; never let your guard down.

## Lesson 83. Use the sword for life not death

Permeating samurai sword culture are the twin concepts of *katsuninken*, the "life-giving sword", and *setsuninto*, the "death-dealing sword". The basic premise is that a sword can be an implement of virtuous creation or evil destruction. There is a time for peace and a time for violence. Without the threat of armed resistance, countries would invade other countries unchecked and criminals would rule the streets. However, it is also a fatal trap to use violence or verbal aggression when it is not appropriate. To do so will quickly turn you from the true path. Many a person has tried to justify their violent behaviour by saying that they were acting in the name of peace. They may succeed in convincing even themselves that they are in the right, but they cannot fool the universe.

The idea of a sword for life and a sword for death is taken from Buddhism, but the lesson is universal. Do not use your martial skills, strength or rank for selfish motives and call it a just cause. The Chinese sages of old stated that the sword was a weapon of ill omen and that it should only ever be used in the direst situation, because the temptation to wield it for one's own benefit was too great. Can you refrain from taking advantage of your own power or can you hold your temper when you feel powerless? That is the test.

**You have to justify your actions, not only to other people but above all to yourself, and you have to be truthful in this. Lying to yourself will throw you off the path, yet it is what we do most of the time.**

## Lesson 84. Contemplate your own death

"Those who cling to life die, while those who cling to death live."

Uesugi Kenshin (1530–1578)

The seventeenth-century strategist Natori Masazumi urged us to "let go of the two swords of life and death", and many other samurai have echoed this idea that a "he who dares wins" or "do or die" attitude is what is needed for victory. Foolhardiness, blood-drunkenness and blind rage are some of the ways to approach battle, but by no means the best. A focused mind with singular dedication is a better approach. It is the same for extreme sports practitioners; those who push the boundary are often at the top of their game. For the *bushi*, facing the prospect of death with calmness made them better fighters, but it did not make them immune to death. It just gave them the mental strength and courage to help them achieve more of their aims before eventually dying.

Your path as a Zen warrior will take you on a journey of death's discovery, to face your own mortality and come to terms with it. You are going to die, that is for sure. You have no idea where you are going in the afterlife, nor does anyone else, but none of that must stop you in the here and now and so death must become your friend.

**Keep death in mind, but not at *all* times; make it a background concept on which to build your life. Focusing on death is macabre, but accepting death is freeing.**

## Lesson 85. Master the art of no-sword

"Swords or spears are weapons to kill others.
However, if a stupid man is so stupid as to have his sword or spear snatched, it will kill him in the end."
*The Book of Ninja*

The term *muto* (無刀) has two basic meanings in the world of swordsmanship. The first meaning is to fight without a sword when the enemy has one, to disarm the opponent and defeat them. It is said that the Yagyu family were experts at this skill. The second meaning of the term is to engage your Zen mind to such a high level that the enemy's sword becomes "no sword". If you are able to overcome any fear you have of the enemy's sword then it becomes irrelevant and ceases to hold any power over you. There is even a sword school called Muto Ryu (無刀流) that is based around this concept.

You can train in the skill of disarming an opponent, but the main lesson here is that your mind is your most powerful tool. A bladed weapon only becomes dangerous when it is wielded by someone who intends to kill. Do we not all have knives in our kitchens, yet how many people are stabbed while cooking? Weapons are items of ill omen, and we should learn how to cope without them.

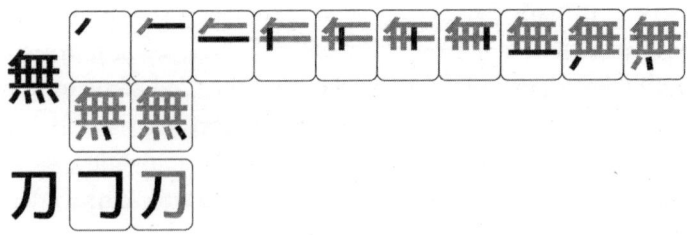

The Japanese term *muto* (無刀) comprises the characters *mu* (無), "absence of" (see lesson 57), and *to* (刀), "sword".

**You may not always be equipped with the physical tools for the situation. Your task is to train your mind to get out of any problem with strategic thinking.**

## Lesson 86. Have compassion for others

"You should develop and master benevolence, starting with the affection and compassion you have for those you associate with."

### *The Book of Samurai*

Compassion is easy when life is easy or when you know that you will benefit from showing kindness. However, compassion becomes more difficult when you are in a bad situation or when you will not gain anything from it, or even suffer because of it. The point of Buddhism is to want less and be happy with less and so it should not irk you if others gain more than you from any situation. This is the foundation of being compassionate. Once you realize that everyone around you *should* have at least as much as you, you will find it easy to help people gain more. Too many people who set out on the spiritual path elevate themselves above others and silently demand more, which only sets them back. Charity and compassion are not genuine if you give only a fraction of what you have. If it does not trouble you to give, then it is no real sacrifice.

**End any obsession you have with gaining more than other people and being further on than those around you. You are trying to escape the bonds of desire, so always be happy for what others gain and gladly give them your time when they need it.**

## Lesson 87. Know that you are not a buddha

You are not an enlightened being and this is not your last incarnation. The Buddhist teachers you admire are not spiritual paragons and your yoga instructor is not a bodhisattva. This is a hard pill to swallow for some people. If the Buddha has seen the truth of the universe and is correct about existence, then we can at least feel confident that we are right to follow his path – but this does not mean that we are anywhere near reaching *nirvana*.

It is OK to make mistakes, as that is the way we learn. So avoid holding on to the illusion that you are close to spiritual perfection. Remember, laughter, fun, drinking, a party here and there are things you should engage with, not disengage from, but always take the middle way. Neither indulge too much nor abstain completely. You live in this world, but you must live in it correctly. Take stock of where you are on this spiritual journey and know that even trying to find the spiritual path is a great step. Do not worry if you ever stray from the path, as it is always possible to change your attitude and get back on track. The path is never too far away. Remember this and you will always move forward.

**Be realistic about your own spiritual progress. Do not be falsely humble, but equally do not over-congratulate yourself. Pride is one of the biggest ways to undermine any spiritual work you have done.**

## Round-up

In part four we considered the various ways in which to interact with an enemy or an opponent. We learned that the best way to wage war is to stop it happening in the first place, but also discussed how to deal with the pressures that any conflict brings and how to hide our rhythms to confuse our opponent. We considered striking distance and whether you should ever strike first, or even if you should strike at all. We also looked at the subtle art of receiving, and how to achieve balance and flow in our movements. We discussed reaction and rationalized the mystery of the Japanese *kiai*, or energy shout. We discussed what to do if you are defeated or if you are victorious, and we looked at the difference between the sword of life and the sword of death. Death is now something which you should be able to contemplate without it becoming a morbid fascination. Finally, you now know that you need compassion for others to move further along the Zen path and have realized that, while there is a long, long way to go before you become a buddha yourself, you are still on the correct road if you are genuinely following the way of the Zen warrior.

# PART 5.
# BECOME A ZEN WARRIOR

We have reached the final leg of our journey through Zen and the samurai sword. What I have to do now is help you piece it all together, to give you something solid to work with on your quest to become a better person. In this fifth section, it is time to map out and clear up the path before you. You will start to think seriously about whether you are here for Zen or for the sword, or just here out of interest. Any of these can be correct, but it is up to you to choose which one fits you best. You will learn to steer clear of complex Zen literature and to practise Zen instead of talking Zen. You will also learn to distinguish between the history of Zen and the practice of Zen, and that being good in one aspect does not make you good at the other. You will learn to recognize sloppy Zen and false Zen, helping you to stay on the path. With these aspects clear and with all illusions removed, we will then home in on what it actually means to be a Zen warrior. We will look at the goal of Zen, spontaneous realization and what this can do for you on your personal journey, and how to ignite and maintain your own spiritual lamp. We will then consider the Daoist aspect of the universe and remind ourselves that the universe is waiting for you and you are not waiting for the universe, and we will finalize our understanding of *nirvana*. Lastly, we will discover how to check our own actions against those of the Buddha himself.

## Lesson 88. Decide whether you want Zen or the sword

The original point of Zen was to remove the analytical side of Buddhism and focus on experience and realization. However, now much of Zen study consists of intellectual debates and questions, meaning that it has turned back toward religious philosophy and away from direct experience. The system is clogged with questions such as what is the Buddha-mind, are we a single being of existence or are we a temporary stream of consciousness, and so on.

Such intellectual debates are acceptable but they should not be given precedence over lived experience. You have to decide what it is you want. Is swordsmanship your primary focus or is the pursuit of enlightenment what drives you? If you say that you are inspired by both, then, in truth, it is probably the sword that you really want. Many dedicated martial artists use Zen as a tool to improve their sword skills, and there is nothing wrong with that. However, others find that when they reach a certain point on the spiritual path, their interest in the sword naturally fades away. There is no problem with a blending of the two disciplines, but it is hard to hold them both equally in your heart. Therefore, it is best to be honest with yourself about what you want now. If not you will start on the wrong foot and may end up far away from your proper destination.

**Always question why you like specific things. Is it for the credibility that goes along with them, or is it because they are something you truly desire? Do not waste time on a path that you think you *should* follow, but that is wrong for you. Tread the path that best suits you from the beginning.**

## Lesson 89. Be aware of and beware of Zen literature

"If you are not skilled in the use of tools, it will be like a Zen monk who knows very well the principles of swordsmanship but is poor at actual sword fighting."

*The Book of Ninja*

Do not put too much trust in the literature of Zen. Like the essence of the Dao, the experience of Zen cannot be written down; it can only be inferred. Zen's sixth patriarch was an illiterate kitchen hand who beat all the Buddhist literati to the most illustrious position in Zen. How did he do this? It is because Zen is an experience, not a logical puzzle. Of course, like the great Way of Daoism, the Zen experience can be described and pathways to finding the Way are given in road signs by others. However, the purpose of Zen is to find that experience yourself, not to read about someone else's discoveries. You can use various forms of literature as a guide – you are doing so right now – but focus on those which ring out with truth and avoid the ones which begin to entangle you. Spiritual truth will never entrap you and it should be simple but profound.

**In Zen things must be light, flowing and free. Never build your spiritual foundation on academic meanderings.**

## Lesson 90. Understand that Zen is now

One lesson you must fully learn is to not idolize the past. There were great *bushi* and great spiritual teachers, but the whole point of Zen is that you are here in the now. A historian's job is to study the past, but any Zen practice must be done in the present. Understanding the history of Zen and practising Zen are two separate things. Yet many Buddhists are stuck in the past and, not only that, are stuck inside of arguments about the past based on arguments from the past. If the Buddha were alive today, he would give you lessons based on social media and video games; he would use the internet as a metaphor and give modern examples of how we get to *nirvana*.

The obsession with historical Zen is not the only problem. Some Zen adherents of the past have been hideous people. Like any organized religion, which is what Zen is, it has chased profit and it has been political; its history is not free of blood. If you believe in Buddhism then you must believe that the Buddha has seen into divinity, the nature of reality, something that you and I cannot see. He was not just a decent man with a few good ideas. Therefore, it is only the Buddha himself who should be followed, not the many thousands of teachers who came after him and who are faint shadows of a greater teacher. Ignore the countless arguments, or at least pay them less heed, and focus on what the Buddha said and make it your code to live by. Only then will you be treading in his footsteps alone.

**Remember that the past may be presented as glorious but it was also far more primitive and bloodthirsty than the present. Even with the troubles of the world today, our time is more peaceful and prosperous than any that has come before it; far more people survive into old age and far fewer die in conflict. To be born now with the opportunity to pursue Zen is to have hit the jackpot of life.**

## Lesson 91. Know the two meanings of Zen

The word Zen has two distinct meanings. Firstly, Zen literally means meditation. When the Buddha sat under his tree, he was performing what would later become known as Zen. Secondly, Zen refers to a religious movement which took hold in China almost a thousand years after the Buddha was alive. There it amalgamated with Daoism before crossing the sea to Japan and establishing itself within the samurai class. In the twentieth century, it became known across the whole world and was updated to fit with modern times and Western culture. The adaptability of Zen is a good thing. It is often thought to be acceptable for the ancient Chinese and then the Japanese to add to Zen and change it, but not for the same thing to happen in countries like the UK and the US. Zen is unique to every individual; it is *your* journey and *your* relationship to the ultimate truth. You have as much right to adapt Zen as the ancient Chinese or Japanese and just as much right as those who sat next to the Buddha. No matter where and when Zen is, it is always only two things: clearing the mind and exploring reality. These two practices alone are all you need to succeed.

**Keep your mind clear, investigate what it means to be human and explore what reality is. Always be kind and compassionate toward others. Know that if you can do these things, there is nothing more you need to do.**

## Lesson 92. Avoid sloppy Zen

Many monks of ancient China and Japan performed sloppy Zen, just like the many fake Zen teachers in the modern day. Sayings like "just chill out", "go with the flow" and "look at it from the Zen perspective" are all phoney. Other indicators of sloppy Zen include practitioners endlessly debating the smallest details of Zen, being rude and stand-offish for no reason, cultivating a "Zen look" that outweighs their actions, and hiding haughtiness behind feigned politeness. Claiming to know secret rituals, spells or pieces of knowledge is another problematic sign. To this day people argue about whether the Buddha passed on secret incantations, magical spells and esoteric doctrine. Perhaps he did, but you can be sure that any secret knowledge offered to you will not have come from him.

My advice to you is to stick to the core aspects of Zen and leave well alone any debatable offshoots. Start by following the Four Noble Truths and the Eightfold Path (see lesson 9) to maintain clarity of mind until you reach some level of realization. This way no one can ensnare you or send you down the wrong path. The more you study and practise the fundamental aspects of Zen, the better you will become at distinguishing between the slop and the real thing.

**The simple way is often the best way. Even though complications can be hard to avoid sometimes, it is best not to seek to complicate your life. Do what is right, not what is best for you, and you will never go wrong.**

## Lesson 93. Use Zen terminology wisely

There will always be a fashion for dropping a buzz word or exotic foreign term into a conversation. This can be both positive and negative. On the positive side, using the right terminology is an efficient way to convey your thoughts to certain audiences. On the negative side, it is easy to become lost in jargon, which, instead of helping your audience, just leads to confusion all round. Many Zen books will give you one example of a term and then use it without explanation again, compounding the problem by doing the same thing with other words over and over again until you are completely lost.

It is normally best to convey your ideas as simply as possible and in your own language, but sometimes you will meet people who do understand the specialist terms and can keep up. The following are a few useful pieces of Zen terminology, but remember that all things can be explained in your own language.

## Fundamental aspects of Buddhism

The term **buddha** means "enlightened one". It is different from a **bodhisattva**, which refers to someone who seeks to become enlightened and become a buddha in the future. The teachings of the Buddha are known in Japanese as *butsudo*, but most people know them as the **Dharma**. Your task is to arrive at an awakening through the *rokkon*, or the six senses. Versions of this awakening are *kensho*, meaning "seeing one's true nature", and *satori*, which is a sudden, intense moment of insight. To become enlightened in these ways, you will need *joriki*, a steady determination to follow the path of Zen training; this path is known as the *kaido*. **Fudo Myo** is a Buddhist deity associated with the important Zen concept of *fudoshin*, the "unaffected mind" (see lesson 59). You will also need to engage in *mushin*, or the "free-flowing mind", along the way (see lesson 57).

## Worship

Communal Zen ceremonies take place in a *zendo*, meaning "hall of Zen", which in some Zen circles and in all Japanese martial arts is known as a *dojo*. A *butsudan* is an altar dedicated to the Buddha and is often used as a place of prayer to your dead relatives. The *jukai* is the ceremony people may go through to become a practitioner, but there are various levels. A *dokusan* is a private interview with a Zen teacher, who might put you through a *mondo*, which is a question-and-answer session. You can go it alone, just like the Buddha did, but if you want guidance you can seek out a *roshi*, or teacher. Most people will benefit from the support of the *sangha* – the Buddhist community – many of whom will chant the **sutras** (verses) together. If you get bored of *zazen* seated meditation with its *kyosaku* hitting stick, then why not try *kinhin*, which is walking meditation? After all this meditation you may need to perform *soji*, which is ritual cleaning. All of this will be pointless if it is not performed with a virtuous mind, known as *toku*. But do not forget to pay your respects to everyone by making the sign of *gassho*: this is to place your hands together in a prayer-like gesture. Finally, lengthy spells of Zen meditation would be unbearable without a *zafu* – a cushion for your bum.

**Try to match your vocabulary to the knowledge level of your audience. Using complex terminology that bamboozles people only shows how foolish you are for not reading the situation correctly.**

## Lesson 94. Break through the logic barrier

Zen bypasses the step-by-step, logical path to enlightenment and replaces it with spontaneous realization. This is not a quick fix, because Zen still focuses very much on hard work and dedication. It is just that you will never get to your destination through the scholar's approach, but instead you must break through the logic barrier to a state of epiphany through experience. You can think logically on the art of Zen, you can think logically on the art of swordsmanship, but thinking will not make you a Zen master nor a master of the blade. Only diligent work will allow you to break through to the next level. Spontaneous realization through extreme hard work is the key. It cannot be replaced with armchair logic.

**You must use Zen when you are wet, cold, hot, bored, stressed, ill, tired ... It is not acceptable to be compassionate, kind and focused only when you are happy, healthy, comfortable and well rested. Zen is constant hard work, but its insights can come suddenly.**

## Lesson 95. Ignite your own lamp of wisdom

There is no one today who has a direct line of transmission back to the Buddha, or even to the patriarchs of Zen. Most historians today agree that some of the patriarchs of Zen were legendary figures and that, even if others did exist in history, the line of secret knowledge claimed to come from them is a later construction, as no writings from the time of the Buddha exist. Just like the king of England today is not really a descendant of the great god Woden, and the Japanese emperor is not a descendant of the sun goddess Amaterasu, Zen masters are not connected to the Buddha in a direct line. If there ever was such a line, it is now frayed beyond practical use.

We do not have a single word written by the Buddha himself. All we have are oral traditions passed down over hundreds of years, which has now turned into over 2,000 years. Along the way there have been countless "masters" who have added to the knowledge of Buddhism and, as you can imagine, not all of them will have had a perfect understanding of the secrets of the universe.

Really, we are all in the same situation as the Buddha at the beginning of his journey, and this is the proper way to be. The Buddha was born into a Hindu world and he was brought up with the teachings of reincarnation, the cycle of life and death, karma and suffering. Likewise, you are exposed to a body of knowledge that claims to hold the key to the secrets of the universe, yet you cannot open the lock. It is for you to find the way through your own experience. Enlightenment may not come to you under a tree as it did the Buddha. It will most definitely not be an experience of full enlightenment in this lifetime, but you may undergo many smaller breakthroughs that will get you on your way to Buddhahood, for that is the goal of humankind.

**Do not rely on others for your spiritual growth or look for their praise and support. Do not lock yourself away in a closed circle of like-minded people. Allow the whole world to give you lessons and take heed of them.**

## Lesson 96. Remember that the universe is waiting for you

The universe is far more powerful than any human. The universe can outwait you; it can outwit you; it has more understanding than you, more than any human. The cosmic rules set in place are waiting for you to move further down the spiritual path before you are given the next challenge. Fate and destiny are not given an allotted timeframe; they are more like way-markers on your spiritual path. You could move through hundreds of lifetimes before you act in the correct way for the next waypoint of destiny to be presented to you. You stand at the Gateless Gate, waiting to move beyond. But as we have seen, the Gateless Gate has no barrier, except in your own mind. It is not the situation around you that is the problem, it is you. You are the problem. No evil empire, no dictatorship, no government, no power on Earth can stand in the way of the universe. When you hit certain realization points then you will move on to the next step. Everything is a test and do not forget it.

**External problems are put there by the universe to test you. Once you have passed the test, you will move on to the next encounter. Until you pass the test, you will be stuck with the same problem all your life. In all cases, the problem lies within you and so you need to look within yourself to solve it.**

## Lesson 97. Revisit the concept of *nirvana*

The goal of Zen is *nirvana*. We have spoken about this several times now but there is always more to say. The word *nirvana* itself originally had negative connotations, as it can denote a desolate "place" where fire and wind do not exist and where the stars have been extinguished, where nothing is or can be, a place devoid of existence. However, within the context of Zen, *nirvana* has two meanings. Firstly, it can mean enlightenment here on Earth, a state of pure bliss. Secondly, it can represent the extinguishing of the "soul", of your identity. When your time in *samsara,* the cycle of life, death and rebirth, is at an end, your suffering and discomfort is over and you are removed from the experience of the universe. No one knows "where" *nirvana* is, or if it is anywhere. All we know is that it is not inside of known existence. Once you have reached *nirvana* you have achieved the final goal.

No one knows the truth of *nirvana*; it cannot be explained in any language because it is not contained within our reality, and language is bound by human understanding of reality. All you need to know about *nirvana* is that it is your goal. What you are aiming to do is leave existence. Be very clear that suicide will not work – that will just bring you straight back here with nothing gained, no matter how many times you do it.

**The end goal of existence is to come to a realization, to experience the universe without a filter. Once you attain the true happiness of *nirvana*, you will move on. Keep to the path of loving-kindness your whole life and you will progress a little bit further in each incarnation.**

## Lesson 98. Aspire to the way of the sage

If the way of the warrior is the lowest spiritual path (see lesson 31), then what is the highest? There is only one high path and it does not belong to any particular religion or sect. It is the way of the sage. To be unbound by complex religious dogma, to be unengaged in controlling human affairs, to not strive to control your own life, to live simply and accept fate, this is the way of the sage. It is to have no plan beyond food and shelter and no longing for the past or desire for the future. Sages deal with whatever the world serves them, working hard within nature to bring benefit to others for no personal gain. Often, they have no fixed home, instead choosing to wander the world. They face both positive and negative events with equanimity. They eat when they can and fast when they cannot.

Neither you nor I is quite there yet. I am writing this book and you are reading it, so together we are bound on a lesser path. All you need to do is test yourself spiritually and build the confidence to break away from human limitations, but remember that the way of the sage is a path you should aspire to tread, even if it is a little way off yet.

**Do not try to become a master of the universe. Instead aim to lead a selfless life with dedication and focus. Effortless action is the key.**

## Lesson 99. Stay on the path

We all stray from the path sometimes. When you can feel this happening to you, look at the following list and ask yourself where you might be falling short:

- Be clean when you can but do not shy away from the dirt acquired through hard work.
- Dress smartly, yet never be overdressed nor underdressed.
- Regulate your physical and mental health by doing all things in moderation – eating, drinking, working, exercising and so on.
- Stretch your mind and body to keep them both supple.
- Look for simplicity in your life.
- Train your mind to have focus.
- Cultivate an attitude of compassion for all living creatures.
- Analyse your own mind and forget about teaching others or the teachings of others.
- Let others deal with their own journey, but give help if you are asked.
- Consider whether you are in the wrong before blaming others.
- If others are wrong, forgive them quickly.
- Contemplate the nature of reality and make both a spiritual and scientific study of the universe, its origins and its rules.

- Know that you are a buddha in waiting and that the universe is waiting for you, so make a start.

If you adhere to the above principles, you will get back on the right path and you can tread forward from there.

**Stay healthy in mind and body, simplify your life, take responsibility for your own actions and focus on clarity of mind. Then wait for the next challenge and accept it.**

## Lesson 100. Sit next to the Buddha

Just imagine yourself sitting next to the Buddha under his tree. What would he tell you to do? Would he tell you to kill, lie, cheat or manipulate in order to get what you want? No, he would not, so do not do those things. When you are struggling with life, sit next to the Buddha in your mind and focus on your journey. Ask yourself how you can maintain kindness to other beings. When things get too complex and discussion groups go round and round in a circle of intellectual masturbation, step back, sit with the Buddha and remember that simplicity is the essence of Zen. There is a massive difference between debates about the history and theory of Zen and the rigorous quest to break through into realization. If you spend your time trying to convince others that you are right, you are doing things the wrong way round.

**Always ask yourself what the Buddha would do. If the answer is different from what you are doing, this tells you that you need to make a change.**

## Round-up

In this fifth section we cleared up some of the problems that dog a Zen follower. Hopefully you will have decided whether you are here for Zen, for the sword, or just out of interest. Even if you have not answered that question yet, keep it in mind. You have been warned about overcomplicating Zen and relying on your knowledge of the history of Zen instead of your ability in Zen. You know to avoid sloppy Zen and false Zen and to focus on spontaneous realization, maintaining the brightness of your own spiritual lamp. You have been reminded that the universe is waiting for you and you are not waiting for it, and that *nirvana* lies beyond existence, if there is such a thing as "beyond". The Buddha has reached *nirvana* and it is the destination that you are aiming for too. So, when in doubt, just ask yourself what the Buddha would do and stay on the path.

We have now come to the end of the five core sections on the way of the Zen warrior, but there is more still ahead. The next section will look at the practicalities of the sword and sword training, using only historical manuals as a guide. At the very end of the book you will find a comprehensive checklist of everything we have covered in the lessons so that you can quickly refresh your memory.

# THE WAY OF THE SWORD AND THE ZEN WARRIOR'S PATH

## The way of the sword

If you are going to become a Zen warrior, you will need to learn how to use a sword. Before you begin, or even if you are an accomplished *kenjutsu* practitioner, understand that Japanese swordsmanship has two main problems. The first is that there are no descriptive records of swordsmanship for the first six centuries of the samurai period, that is roughly between the years 1000 and 1600. We simply do not know how they fought. The most we have are interesting quotes from literature and some skill lists, which tell us almost nothing about what the samurai actually did. The second issue is that, even though some sword schools have existed since this dark period and have to some extent retained the same named skills, research has shown that most of those skills have changed dramatically over time. Therefore, while practitioners of old sword schools today are often part of an unbroken transmission of swordsmanship, there is little to no doubt that the sword skills they teach are drastically different from those of the original masters.

So we are at an almost total loss to know how the samurai fought in the earlier part of their existence. What we do know is how the later samurai fought, or at least we can glimpse into their ways. The swordsmanship in this chapter represents what was being practised by some schools between the years 1600 and 1868, which is when imperial rule was restored to Japan, leading to the abolition of the samurai class soon after.

The majority of the sword basics given in this section are taken from the historical scroll the Heiho Kadensho (兵法家伝書), or

"Secret Military Ways and Traditions of Our Family", written by Yagyu Munenori in 1632. This is the foundation text for the samurai sword school known as Yagyu Shinkage Ryu, an ideal school for us to focus on because it embodies the fusion of spiritual beliefs and martial arts that became widespread in the later samurai period. Therefore, in this section you will find the principles of what might be termed Zen swordsmanship. What you will not find here are details of all the original sword combinations or *kata*. A filmed demonstration of the full system can be found on YouTube under the title "All Yagyu Shinkage Ryu Kata" on my channel Samurai Martial Arts Real Training (S.M.A.R.T.). This video has been pinned on the main page. You can also follow this channel for further sword instruction.

## The three basic principles

"Out of ten parts: three-tenths is in the mind; three-tenths is in the hand; three-tenths is in the sword; and one-tenth is in momentum. Remember that even if you have a master-class sword, unless you use mind, hand and momentum you will not make a cut."

*The Book of Samurai*

There are three major points to keep in mind when you engage with swordsmanship:

1. Your stance is a natural defence against an enemy attack, so keep it low but still allow for smooth movement.
2. Your hands and feet must move fluidly and without awkwardness.
3. Your sword should move as a part of your body.

Keep these three points in mind when involved in the practice of *kenjutsu* – Japanese swordsmanship.

**Japanese swords are not uniform – their style, shape and weight changed over centuries of warfare and peace.**

## The five basic practices

"When in single combat, attack from a lower position. … An opponent who attacks you from a higher position tends to make mistakes. For example, if he attempts to strike you with his sword as soon as he has drawn it, he may misjudge the distance."

*The Book of Samurai*

There are five basic principles which you should maintain throughout a sword fight. Of course, movements change during a fight but doing the following will strengthen your stance:

1. Hold your body side on.
2. Set your shoulder at the same height as your opponent's fists.
3. Use your fists as a form of shield between yourself and your opponent.
4. Extend your left arm and slightly bend your right (or vice versa if you are left-handed).
5. Shift your weight somewhat toward your forward knee.

Research shows that the original Yagyu Shinkage Ryu used a right-foot-forward stance for most of their basic fighting skills. While this may change depending on the *kata*, most of your time will be spent with your right foot forward while adhering to the above five principles.

**Japanese swords are today divided into very strictly defined categories. However, in the past these specifications varied.**

## The three basic stances

There are three basic stances used in this school, although there are other options for specific situations. You will notice that the five basic principles described in the last section are used in each stance, but the hands are set at different levels. In Japanese the three stances are known as *jodan* ("high stance"), *chudan* ("middle stance") and *gedan* ("low stance"). In each of these, your form stays the same. All that changes is the position of the arms and the sword.

*jodan*    *chudan*    *gedan*

**Japanese swords are on the whole divided into the following types: *tachi* ("great sword"), *katana* ("longsword"), *wakizashi* ("short sword") and *chiisa-gatana* ("dagger").**

# The three basic cuts

Samurai sword fights were not won with single slaying cuts or long, overdrawn slashes. Fighting would have been tight, sleek, minimal and close. Initially, cuts would be small and directed, before opening up into medium sized hacks, and then, only when absolutely sure, the cautious *bushi* would extend to a powerful slash to finish off their enemy. Smaller cuts were a part of tactics; larger and more powerful attacks were for finishing.

Practise the following three cuts to enlarge your repertoire.

**I Small swipe.** This is to make your enemy move. When close to the enemy, make a small forward circular motion with your hands to create a small circle cut with the tip of your blade. Direct this small circle cut toward the enemy's wrist or elbow. This will force them to move so that you can move into advantage.

**2 Push–pull cut.** This is used when the enemy is at a disadvantage, even if it is a small one. Push the hands forward and pull the cut backwards after finding and landing on the target. This cut still has circular motion but is pulled back heavily to deepen the cut.

**3 Heavy downward cut.** This is to finish your enemy off. Bring down the sword with all your might, after you have played the opponent into a disadvantageous position. This very heavy cut is known as *kiriotoshi* (切落) and has great power and force put into it.

Japanese swords were originally straight, modelled after older Chinese swords. The swords were later made longer and curved. These curved swords were then exported to China and adopted by the Chinese.

## Striking

"When striking with the sword, keep the inside of the hand relaxed, hold the hilt tightly with the rear fingers, push slightly forward and then cut by pulling. Hold your breath on the strike. To perform this, hold this action as a feeling in your mind."

*The Book of Samurai*

The following are the three main types of strike in combat situations:

1. A mutual strike, which is something to be avoided
2. Striking the enemy's hands from below when they raise their sword

3. Striking the enemy's hands from above when they lower their sword.

This illustration shows the strike from below (left) and the strike from above (right). As the mutual strike is discouraged, it is not shown here.

Analysis of old sword manuals shows that the majority of first strikes toward the enemy are aimed at the hands. This is because once an enemy's hands have been damaged it is hard for them to continue the fight, and also because the hands are the easiest part to reach.

The following are further points on the art of striking:

- Sword cuts are done in a single beat.
- Sword cuts are never more than one foot in reach, this is the measurement of the movement of the arms.
- You will need to be in close and at the correct distance before you can make your attack.
- Most sword cuts are not full attacks; they are lighter probing cuts. However, when you have the opportunity, perform the full *kiriotoshi* blow, which is a hard and decisive downward blow.
- When the enemy raises their sword from a middle or lower guard into a higher position, move in and cut their hands from below.

- Sometimes use broad, long strokes, while at other times use short, chopping strokes.
- If the enemy uses broad strokes, respond with short strokes.
- If the enemy uses short strokes, respond with broad strokes.
- Sometimes when the enemy strikes out, instantly strike them in return.
- After you have hit the enemy, put pressure on and do not let them lift their sword. Keep the momentum going.
- After a hit, push on with up to five extra strikes. Do this with successive beats without any gap between them. This will drive the enemy into submission.
- If you are close enough, kick your enemy (see illustration).

**kick**

Japanese swords can be slung either blade edge up or blade edge down. *Tachi* are mainly slung blade edge down, and *katana* blade edge up. However, you can find historical examples of this being reversed.

## Movement

"When the opponent is moving in toward you, you will make a deeper cut than expected. Conversely, when you are following up on the opponent as he is withdrawing, you will most likely end up striking with only the tip."

**The Book of Samurai**

When you are training, understand and practise the following aspects of your swordsmanship:

- *Ken* (懸) means to attack quickly and swiftly. Therefore, sometimes you should adopt a stance and attack with controlled speed.
- *Tai* (待) means to wait for the enemy to attack. Therefore, sometimes you should adopt a stance and wait.
- Sometimes you should have no set stance at all and just move freely.
- Your movement should be light and not heavy.
- The seat of your intention and movement should be from the waist down. All movement comes from the bottom half of your body; the upper half of your body performs strikes and blocks.
- Connect the movement of the lower half of your body to the movement of your hands so that you move as one with your sword.
- Steps should be done in a calm way, neither fast nor slow.
- Move in close without striking and force the enemy to strike so that you can strike them as they move.
- When the enemy moves, you should move with fluidity into the correct position so that you have the advantage.
- Do not maintain the same rhythm because the opponent will match it and guess your next movements. It is best to be out of rhythm with the enemy.
- Take your time in the combat as you form your strategy.

Train in the above until all of your movements and decisions come instinctively.

**Japanese swords were not all equal in quality. Like modern cars, some were high-performance models and some were equivalent to factory-line productions.**

## Distance

Observe the following rules on distance until they become second nature:

- The distance between you and the enemy will be around six feet: three feet for your sword and three feet for theirs. Once your sword tips cross, you are in danger.
- Keep a constant distance and allow the enemy to be just out of reach but not so far away that you are no longer engaged with them.
- Allow the enemy to get close enough to strike out but not hit. Next use their new position to attack them at advantage.
- Sometimes move a few inches inside of the enemy's range to provoke them.
- Sometimes close in and get close to the enemy's body. Do this if they will not react to your feints.

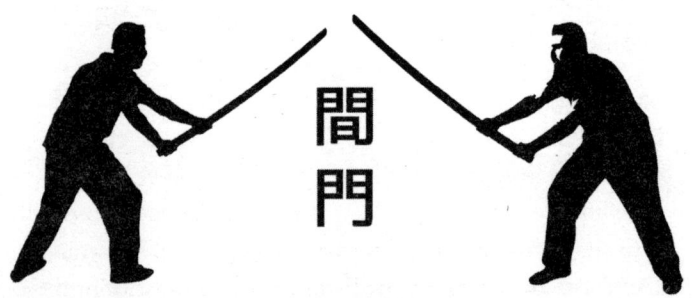

*kenmon*-distancing

## Observation

One of the great secrets of fighting with a sword is to avoid looking directly at your opponent with focused direct vision. Old sword manuals talk about the various places to look when facing an enemy. The use of peripheral vision (see lesson 39) is more important than watching what the enemy is doing. Therefore:

- Focus your eyes mainly on the enemy's hands. By doing this you will see their shoulders in your peripheral vision and so you will see the initial movement of their strikes.
- Look out for a tightening of the hands or a stiffening of the elbow, which are indicators of an impending attack.
- Focus on the elbows when the enemy is in the upper position or when they are going to strike from above.
- Focus on the enemy's chest when you have clashed and are up close.

Remember to change your focus depending on where you are in the fight.

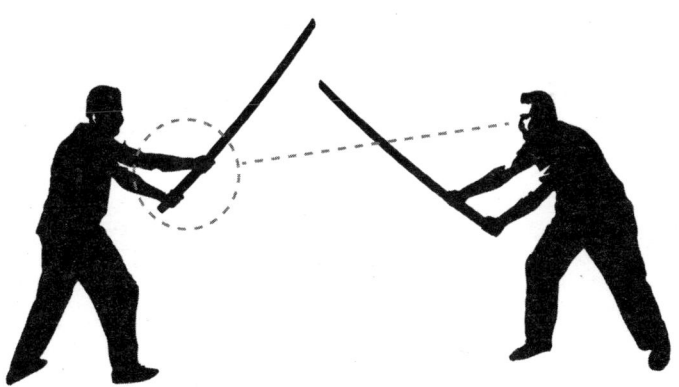

**Japanese swords were treated in different ways. Some would have been highly polished; others would have been dull and sharpened with moleskins filled with stone, causing scratches along the blade.**

# The philosophy of sword fighting

"In a one-to-one combat between warriors, take the enemy's substantial mind and make it insubstantial. In this way, you can defeat them."

*The Book of Samurai*

The following points summarize the fighting philosophy of the Yagyu family:

- Observe the enemy to try to learn what they will do.
- Try to force the enemy to make the first move.
- Use deception to confuse the enemy into making a mistake.
- Force the enemy into change, then take advantage of that change.
- You can wait for the enemy to attack, or you can attack directly.
- Your body can attack while your sword waits (this means that you can make your stance and movement threatening without actually making a strike).
- Your body can attack while your mind waits (this means that you can make feints a part of your arsenal while you withhold your attack).
- Appear calm at all times, even if below the surface you are in full active mode.
- Excellence is found in blending the concepts of attacking and waiting.
- Focusing too much on any one thing will cause you to lose because your mind will become stuck.
- If you land a strike, focus your mind on what the enemy is doing but keep your thoughts agile. If you spend time thinking about the blow you have just landed, it will prevent you from reacting properly. Just move on.

## The way of no-sword

"Drawing the sword is weak, while not drawing is strong. Those who have a courageous mind will not draw without care; this is what should be kept in mind about confrontations."

*The Book of Samurai*

One of the most prestigious concepts in swordsmanship is that of *muto* (無刀), "no-sword", which we first encountered in lesson 85. The Yagyu clan were said to be masters of this style. The following points summarize their teachings on the matter.

- You do not have to take the opponent's sword in this skill. Simply avoiding their strikes is one way to perform *muto*.
- Sometimes you should disarm the opponent and take their sword.
- Part of the secret of this skill is proper distancing.
- To disarm someone, you have to be within their cutting range.
- Disarming can be done by going under the attacking cut.
- If the enemy is focusing on not letting you disarm them, do not try to do it. You will fail.
- However, if the enemy's focus is on cutting you, try disarming them.
- It is acceptable to use other implements in a sword fight, even if it is just a fan. Pick up anything you can if you are unarmed.

**Japanese swords were not too expensive for wartime samurai. Many samurai had multiple sword sets and many were left over from the wars. Even peasants used to own and carry Japanese swords until Toyotomi Hideyoshi banned the practice in the late sixteenth century. That is why it is more accurate to refer to these swords as Japanese swords than samurai swords.**

The above ten lessons constitute the basics of sword fighting according to the Yagyu family secret scrolls. While there are many different sword schools in Japan, this is one of the most prestigious. On your path to becoming a Zen warrior, instil these aspects into your unconscious mind so that they come out instinctively in your training.

## The Zen warrior's path

You must be clear in your mind that this book is only a guide to the road ahead. The real quest starts after you have finished reading. If you intend to take up the sword, be it literally or metaphorically, your journey will be laden with opportunities to convert the lessons I have given you into real-life skills. Alternatively, this could become just another self-help book on your shelf … but I hope not. Reading and thinking constitute only a small percentage of your training path. Control over body and mind will make up most of the work.

Now that you are approaching the end of the book, you may be a little wiser about Zen and have a deeper understanding of Japanese swordsmanship, but have no idea how to collate all this information. Do not worry, I have done that for you. This next section provides checklists that I hope you will find useful for both sword and Zen training. It will help you to crystallize your understanding and avoid any pitfalls, and make it clear what you will actually have to do in practical terms. If you are ever stuck, come back to this section; it will always be here to keep you focused on the path you are to follow.

## Fundamental points

- A correct state of mind at all times is your primary goal.
- Control your desires, but do not suppress them entirely.
- You should have the skills of an expert but the free, unhindered mind of a beginner.

- You should not wait to engage with difficult things or try things that are beyond your level.
- Overall, you should act with focused and controlled speed when in emergency situations. Do not flit about but instead be direct.
- In both Zen and swordsmanship, over-focusing and focusing on not focusing will cause you trouble.
- Whenever you are defeated, go on the offensive straight away.

## Mind and body

- Cultivating a healthy body and mind is the first step toward perfection.
- The human brain functions thanks to a combination of chemical and electrical systems.
- The mind is divided into the conscious mind, the subconscious mind and the unconscious mind. The last of these is also known as the inner-mind.
- The conscious mind is your thoughts.
- The inner-mind thinks for you and is beyond your control.
- The term adaptive unconscious refers to the inner-mind's ability to react instinctively to danger.
- Your eyes function in different ways depending on the situation.
- Your mind will move between conscious and unconscious actions and you need to use the correct type of action at the correct time.
- Muscle memory, gained through many hours of dedicated practice, is what makes you proficient in any physical activity.
- If you are in a situation that calls for fast action, conscious thinking is redundant. Your inner-mind should take over and cause your body to react correctly. This will only happen if you have trained sufficiently.
- You have six senses, including the sixth sense of intuition. Use them all.

- The sixth sense has not yet been scientifically proven, but there is proof enough that a heightened mind is a high-functioning mind.
- The mind is like a mirror or a gem. It is always clean below the layers of dirt and so your task is to polish it.
- If you trust in your own training, trust that your own mind will save you.

## Samurai overview

- *Bushi* is an older Japanese term meaning warrior.
- The terms *bushi* and samurai are interchangeable most of the time.
- The way of the warrior is the lowest of the spiritual paths (the way of the sage is the highest), but it is still a worthy path to follow.
- The concept of *shuhari* divides *bushi* training into three stages: learning basic individual skills; being able to use these skills in combination; and being able to go beyond these skills and achieve mastery.
- There are four ways the samurai used to respond to a situation: meet it with strength; avoid it with softness; stand rigid and firm; or be flexible enough to manipulate it.
- Buddhism was in Japan before the samurai class existed and it helped create the samurai identity.
- Historically Zen was a violent and political tool used by the samurai.
- *Dojo* culture is the idea that as samurai settled in castle towns at the end of the time of wars, they formed groups and schools to pass on military knowledge.

### Living like the samurai

- To live like the samurai, there are various steps you can take.
- You should test yourself in the world, to discover your limits and weaknesses.

- You should keep an eye out for the tell-tale signs of future problems and try to avert trouble before it arises.
- You should own a sword, even if it is only for symbolic purposes.
- You should have a sense of thankfulness toward people who have helped you in some way.
- You should have a grasp of cultural matters, including current affairs, history, philosophy, poetry and the arts.
- You should read military literature, including military classics and chronicles.
- You should dedicate yourself to an art, organization or skill. Become an expert in something.
- You should wear practical, simple yet stylish clothes.

## Swordsmanship

- Japanese swordsmanship is known as *kenjutsu*.
- No one knows how the samurai fought before the year 1600.
- Swordsmanship went through observable changes in later samurai times.
- Zen and the sword only became connected in these later times of peace.
- Japanese swords were used by other classes, not just the samurai.
- Not all Japanese swords were holy items. The idea of praying or bowing to your sword is relatively modern.
- You do not need a *dojo* to train in; you can train wherever there is space to swing a sword.
- Train outside if you prefer, or ask a local priest if you can train at a church or temple in exchange for a small donation.
- Success in swordsmanship, like any activity, depends on switching between the conscious and unconscious minds.
- *Kata* is a choreographed fight between two participants to help each person build up their unconscious responses.
- *Waza* refers to the practice of a single skill in swordsmanship.

- *Kenmon* and *maai* are both terms that refer to distance in swordsmanship.
- *Atari* means the middle point, the transition between two opposites, such as day into night. It refers to the middle of any movement you make.
- You will have to decide for yourself if it is better to spar or not to spar as a part of your training.
- At the start of combat your mind is in its logical state, but when the action is on, your inner-mind takes over.
- Never look at your opponent directly; look at their hands, elbows, chest or even look behind them. This engages your peripheral vision.
- The concept of *muhyoshi* is to have no discernible rhythm, to flow like liquid from one move to the next and to be at the correct place at the correct time.
- Sometimes you have to initiate combat. In the old world, knowing when to initiate and when not to initiate was sometimes the difference between life and death.
- Sometimes you have to block directly; at other times you have to receive and move the enemy's blade out of the way.
- The *kiai* is an energetic shout that can give you courage or help you act in the moment. It is not magical or spiritual but it has a real effect.
- The term "life-giving sword" means to use violence in a way to benefit society, whereas the "death-dealing sword" refers to unjustifiable violence. They are also terms used for martial arts moves in the samurai school Yagyu Shinkage Ryu.
- In *kenjutsu* the skill of *muto* is to go into a sword fight without a sword and be able to take your opponent's sword from them or to gain victory without a sword.

## Religions overview

- The idea of what exists beyond reality is indescribable.
- The Way or the Dao is the underlying essence of the universe. It provides a spiritual path for you to follow.
- Daoism deals with the universe and your place in it.
- Buddhism deals with your inner-mind and spiritual progression.
- Confucianism deals with how you behave in society.
- Shinto deals with connecting to the past, our ancestors and the realm of the gods.
- You should have a basic knowledge of religions and their history and philosophy, including Buddhism in general and Zen in particular.

## Buddhism

- The term buddha means "enlightened one" and Buddhism is the path the original historical Buddha prescribed.
- Buddhism contains a set of cosmic laws and the rules for leaving behind continuous existence within the known universe.
- Buddhism teaches us to take the middle path, which means to avoid extremes.
- Religious concepts such as karma and reincarnation existed before the Buddha and Buddhism.
- The truth of Buddhism is said to have been passed down through the patriarchs of Zen.
- Some teachings are said to come from the Buddha himself; others are from people who came after him.
- The Buddha is the greatest Buddhist, so do not over-invest in the teachings of those who came after him. Focus on his words above all others'.
- Buddhism is divided into two main branches: Theravada, which focuses on the earliest Buddhist teachings; and Mahayana, which takes a more esoteric approach.

- The *sangha* is the worldwide Buddhist community, to which Buddhists can turn locally for support.
- *Samsara* is the cycle of life, death and rebirth within reality. You are stuck in this loop and your aim is to get out.
- You could be reincarnated as a human, a spirit, an animal or even in another dimension.
- You will continue to be reincarnated until you pay off your karmic debt and experience the Great Realization, which will lead to your soul being extinguished.
- Enlightenment is to have the Great Realization and to exit the cycle of life, death and rebirth.
- The Buddha-mind or Buddha-nature is the divinity inside you which is hidden behind layers of thought-dirt. Your job is to clean your mind so that your Buddha-nature can shine through.
- Compassion for other life forms is an important quality to develop in your Buddhist journey.
- Compassion and charity are only real if you do not benefit from any kind actions you perform and if what you give is hard for you to spare.
- A bodhisattva is a person who has made a serious commitment to becoming a buddha. In some Buddhist sects these people are seen as having supernatural abilities.
- *Nirvana* is to never again be reborn inside of reality, and as such it is your final goal and destination. It cannot be described; it might not even exist. The fact that it is outside of known existence is the whole point. Never get bogged down trying to imagine *nirvana*.
- Buddhism's principal teachings are the Four Noble Truths, the Eightfold Path and the Six Perfections.

## Four Noble Truths

- The first of the Four Noble Truths is that you will experience discomfort and suffering in your life.

- The second is that this discomfort and suffering is of your own making.
- The third is that discomfort and suffering reduce when you have less attachment to earthly things.
- The fourth is that you need to follow the Eightfold Path.

## Eightfold Path

- The first aspect of the Eightfold Path is to understand the reality of suffering and discontent.
- The second is to have only positive ideas.
- The third is to be positive in all you say.
- The fourth is to do only things that do not harm others.
- The fifth is to not do anything that is negative to others.
- The sixth is to put effort in the right places and think positively.
- The seventh is to look after your mental health.
- The eighth is to have dedication and focus of mind.

## Six Perfections

- The first of the Six Perfections is generosity to others.
- The second is self-discipline.
- The third is patience.
- The fourth is diligence.
- The fifth is concentration and meditation.
- The sixth is wisdom.

# Zen

- Zen is an experience above all things, a path to spiritual realization.
- Zen has two goals: mental clarity and then realization of the true nature of reality.
- Zen is about you living now and dealing with this moment.

- Zen is for everyone at any time and at any place. It does not belong to any one nation. It has travelled through time and space without a home. You are its home.
- Zen should be practised, not preached. Focusing too much on academic Zen or Zen history is the wrong path.
- Zen is only one of many ways to reach enlightenment.
- Zen is not Japanese. It started with the Buddha in India, then travelled through China before crossing the sea to reach Japan.
- You should not practise traditional Zen without first understanding the basics of Buddhism.
- Before reaching Japan, Zen was influenced by Daoism and other Chinese thought systems.
- Zen was transmitted in Japan through powerful people who had wealth and power. In this way, it became associated with the military government.
- Zen history and philosophy are only small parts of Zen. Being knowledgeable in either does not make you a good  practitioner.
- Zen terminology is sometimes corrupted by bad translation.
- Koans are unanswerable statements and riddles, which, if used correctly, can help you make a spiritual breakthrough. They are not logical debates.
- Understand that detachment is not the same as non-attachment. Detachment is to actively move away from things; non-attachment is to engage with things but not hold on to them.
- Delusion is to not see the world as it is; it means allowing your mind to twist what is really happening.
- *Mushin* is translated as "no-mind", but it does not mean mindlessness. It is the absence of conscious thought or the presence of the unconscious mind.
- *Mukei* is translated as "no-form", but it does not mean formlessness. It is the idea that someone is so well trained that you cannot perceive their form.

- Form within the formless means that, while things seem in disarray on the surface, expert ability can be called upon at any time.
- The Gateless Gate is a mental image of a gateway without a door in it. You believe you cannot go forward, but that is just an illusion. No one is hindering your spiritual path but you.
- *Fudoshin* means to have an unaffected mind. Nothing outside yourself should change your thoughts.
- A Zen warrior must not be changed by any internal or external pressures. Even if something kills you, do not let it affect you.
- You must face up to the reality of death. This does not have to be macabre, but to ignore death is to fail on the Zen path.
- The Ten Ox-Herding Pictures provide a visual map to show you the way to enlightenment and to help you identify each stage.
- The concept of *muto* in Zen is to have no fear of enemy aggression or weapons.

## Meditation

- The word Zen is a translation of older Chinese and Indian words meaning "absorption" or "meditation". Saying "I am going to do Zen" is the same as saying "I am going to meditate."
- Meditation is simply to sit and clear the mind. Nothing more.
- You do not need a special place to train in Zen. You can do this anywhere.
- *Zazen* is seated meditation.
- Own a cushion to sit on in meditation.
- To meditate, set a timer, get comfortable and control your mind.
- In meditation you can engage in focused meditation, which is to concentrate on something like an image or your breathing, or you can engage in open monitoring, which is to allow thoughts to come and go until they have been exhausted and you have control of them.

- In meditation, once you have a quiet mind you can concentrate and focus on the nature of reality, which will help you break through to see universal truths.
- Controlling the mind and seeing universal truths are the primary goals of meditation.
- Liberation is complete control of your mind.

## Final points

- If you are ever lost on your Zen path to enlightenment, stop and simplify things. This will get you back on track.
- The universe is waiting for you to make your move. Do not wait for the universe.
- Above all, remember that the solutions to any problems you encounter lie within you.

# NEXT STEPS

Unless you have flicked to the end, you will have now fully consumed the chapters of this book and looked over the checklists. You are almost ready to take action, to set off on your journey. So what next? The first thing you need to do is ask yourself one important question: are you a Zen warrior? It is totally acceptable to say no, because this path is not for everyone. You may not wish to follow the way of the Zen sword. Alternatively, you may wish to set the swordsmanship aspect to one side and focus your Zen training on another pursuit, or you may just want to study the reality of medieval combat. If any of the above applies to you, then know that reading this book has not been a waste of time. It may, in fact, have pushed you to the next level, to a new place in your life. My only wish is that you cherish this book as a turning point, if it indeed proves to be one.

If you have decided that the path of Zen swordsmanship is just where you want to be, then understand that practice is your next step. Action, action, action. If you do not train in swordsmanship or you do not engage in Zen, then you are missing the point. Having made this decision, it would be beneficial to reread this book each year to polish the dust from your mirror-mind. What you should definitely *not* do is just turn to the next feel-good book, which is a mistake many people make. Now is the time to actually do the work. Take your sword, be it real or wooden, and go through the swordsmanship training in this book. Practise hitting a target, blocking, striking and countering.

For more training exercises in swordsmanship, follow me on my YouTube channel: Samurai Martial Arts Real Training @SamuraiCombatives. If you have done all of the above and your thirst has still not been slaked, then there is more. I hope you will not mind if I recommend you back up this training with one of my other volumes, *How to Be a Modern Samurai*. This will give you a structure that will help you to embrace the *bushi* lifestyle. *How to Be a Modern Samurai* is also available in audio format.

Combining these aspects will give you a life framework, a practical guide to both swordsmanship and military strategy, accompanied by a grounding in Zen. If there is anyone left who still has burning energy inside their hearts, you can personally join my samurai school of war, Natori-Ryu (see page 169). For everyone, no matter how involved you are along this path, I wish you all the best in finding stability within the chaos of life. Lift the dark shroud from your eyes and look for realization.

# POSTSCRIPT

## March 2025

Not long after I had submitted the first draft of this book, I was driving south on the A1 road in eastern England when my Zen reactions were tested to the full. From my right, a car came screeching past at about 70 miles an hour; it was on its side, sparks and glass flying, its wheels saying hello. It then flipped onto its roof and started to tumble over and over like something from a James Bond car chase. There was no other vehicle between mine and this rogue car flying in front of me. With extreme calmness I gently slowed down, even instinctually indicating to go around the car as it continued to flip its way toward the ditch. Then, in true English gent fashion, I pulled over at the side of the road to offer assistance to the driver of the crashed car. As a group of us pulled him out, I observed that, though he was covered in blood, he was able to stand. I concluded that he would be alright and so drove on my way as others fussed about him waiting for the ambulance.

Not once did my heart falter, not once did I exclaim or show any sign of distress. My inner-mind took over and caused my body to react in the perfect way for that situation.

## July 2025

Could it be possible that after almost 30 years of largely uneventful driving, two out-of-the-ordinary incidents would take place within the time it took to edit this book? But as Daniel Culver, my editor at Watkins, sent me the page-set version of the book, I was driving along a quiet English country road, my one-year-old son Arthur in the back and my fiancée Emma in the front, when ahead of us a car coming the opposite way started to swerve over to our side of the road. Quickly it become obvious that there would soon be a head-on collision unless I took immediate action. My mind focused without thinking and my actions quickly and efficiently steered our car mostly off the road and onto the grass verge. Holding on as we bounced on the rough ground, I came back on the road, while the other car casually returned to its own side.

To this day I do not know if it was a joyrider or just someone not paying attention. But the universe could not be clearer: "Antony, the teachings are correct. Now pick up your sword and train!"

What I have learned from these two events is that if I spent as much time practising with a sword as I do driving up and down the country, then my swordsmanship would be better. I feel ashamed of my lack of effort in kenjutsu. But at least I know from first-hand experience that the lessons in this book work, and I wanted you to know this too.

Let us hope that this is the end of my automotive adventures and life returns to normal. Trust in your training.

Antony Cummins

# SELECTED GLOSSARY

The following contains the key terms used in this book, as well as a small number of additional terms to help develop your understanding more fully.

**adaptive unconsciousness** – a term coined by psychologist Daniel Wegner to describe reactions and decision-making done without conscious thought

*atari* (中り) – the moment or space between movements; the transition point between opposing states (e.g. night and day)

**Bodhidharma** – the 28th patriarch of Zen and the first patriarch of the Chinese lineage (having travelled to China from India)

*bushi* (武士) – class of medieval Japanese warrior more popularly known as samurai (侍)

**Dao** (道) – also known as the Way, the unobservable, indescribable structure-intelligence upon which the universe rests and which created all things

**Dharma** – the teachings of the Buddha passed down as Buddhism

*dukkha* – suffering, discomfort, unhappiness

**explicit memory** – memory that requires a conscious effort to use; it comprises episodic memory (past events) and semantic memory (general knowledge)

*fudoshin* (不動心) – literally "unaffected mind", meaning to be unaffected by any external influence

**Gateless Gate** – see *mumonkan*

*giri* (義理) social and legal obligations that lead you to feel indebted to someone (see also *on*)

*go* (剛) – rigid state of mind (see *shido*)

*heijoshin* (平常心) – to maintain a calm mind under stress

**implicit memory** – unconscious, non-verbal memory of skills and habits, such as riding a bicycle

**inner-mind** – the term used in this book for the unconscious mind

**isshin furan** (一心不乱) – singlemindedness without confusion

**ju** (柔) – flexible state of mind (see *shido*)

**jyaku** (弱) – soft, passive state of mind (see *shido*)

**kan** (家) – house or clan; when used as a suffix, it denotes an organization or, in martial arts, an individual *dojo* within a school

**kan** (観) – listening or "seeing" with the mind, in contrast to the concept of *ken*

**kanji** (漢字) – the main Japanese alphabet adopted from China

**kannen** (観念) – seeing through your own thoughts

**karateka** (空手家) – person who studies karate

**kata no uke** (形ノ請) – perception of form

**katsujinken** (活人剣) – literally "life-giving sword", meaning to exercise violence in order to preserve the lives of others

**ken** (懸) – to attack swiftly

**ken** (見) – seeing with the eyes, in contrast to *kan*

**kendoka** (剣道家) – person who practises the sport of *kendo*

**kenjutsu** (剣術) – Japanese swordsmanship

**kenmon** (間門) – the distance between two opponents in martial arts (see also *maai*)

**kensei** (剣聖) – sword saint, the most prestigious title given only to those who have truly mastered the art

**kenshi** (剣士) – scholar of the sword

**kensho** (見性) – enlightenment by seeing your own nature

**kenzen ichinyo** (剣禅一如) – Japanese saying which means "Zen and the sword are one"

**kokoro no uke** (心ノ請) – perception using the mind

**kyo** (強) – strong state of mind (see *shido*)

**kyojutsu** (虚実) – art of deceiving an opponent by presenting unreality as reality

**maai** (間合い) – concept of distancing in martial arts (see also *kenmon*)

**Mahayana** – one of the two main branches of Buddhism; it contains more arcane and esoteric teachings than the other branch, Theravada

*manako* (眼ノ請) – perception using the eyes

*mu* (無) – concept describing the potential for something to exist, in contrast to *u* (有), which describes something that actually exists

*muhyoshi* (無拍子) – imperceptible timings and unobservable rhythm

*mumonkan* (無門関) – Japanese term translated into English as the Gateless Gate; a spiritual obstacle within you that blocks your path toward enlightenment

*mushin* (無心) – absence of restrictive thinking

*muto* (無刀) – to be without a sword yet attain victory

*nembutsu* (念仏) – Buddhist chant which is said over and over during meditation to help gain enlightenment

*on* (恩) – concept of thankfulness; debt to be repaid for past actions (see also *giri*)

*ryu* (流) – suffix normally attached to different martial arts schools (e.g. Yagyu Shinkage Ryu)

*samsara* – cycle of life, death and rebirth

**samurai** (侍) – class of medieval Japanese warrior also known as *bushi* (武士)

*satori* (悟り) – enlightenment by sudden realization

*satsuninto* (殺人刀) – literally the "death-dealing sword", meaning unjustifiable violence

*shido* (四道) – concept of the four basic states of mind, to be switched between according to the situation: *ju* (柔), meaning "flexibility"; *go* (剛), meaning "rigidity"; *kyo* (強), meaning "strength"; and *jyaku* (弱), meaning "softness"

*shinkan* (心鑑) – the model mind, the perfection of self

*shinku* (心 空 ) – the emptied mind

*shoshin* (初心) – the beginner's mind, a free mental state where thoughts do not inhibit natural reactions

*shugyosha* (修 行 者) – "person in training", one who aspires to conform with the Way

*shuhari* (守破離) – three-layered approach to training, consisting of: *shu* (守), learning individual skills; *ha* (破), combining individual skills; and *ri* (離), breaking away from the fundamentals and creating something new based on true mastery

*suigetsu* (水月) – true reflection, often presented as the moon reflected in water

*tai* (待) – to wait for the enemy to attack

*tanren* (鍛錬) – perfection through constant training

*teuchi* (手討) – an order to kill an associate or fellow samurai

**Theravada** – one of the two main branches of Buddhism; it focuses on the earliest Buddhist teachings

**thin slicing** – term developed by psychologists Nalini Ambady and Robert Rosenthal to refer to humans' ability to reach valid judgements based on a snapshot, or thin slice, of information

*u* (有) – existence, in contrast to *mu* (無), which is the potential for existence or absence of existence

*ukemi* (請身) – the process of receiving

**Way** – see Dao

# JOIN A SAMURAI SCHOOL

Founded in the sixteenth century, the Natori-Ryu samurai school taught the military ways of the Natori family who served the famous Japanese warlord Takeda Shingen. The school was redeveloped and expanded in the seventeenth century by Natori Masazumi, who was also known as Issui-sensei. The original school closed its doors in the late nineteenth century, but, after extensive research and blessings from the Natori family, Natori-Ryu was reopened on 5 May 2013 with Antony Cummins as the project leader. The collected Natori-Ryu scrolls dating from the seventeenth century have been translated into English and published in the *Book of Samurai* series (Watkins), enabling students around the world to study these authentic *bushi* teachings.

For those interested in studying the way of the samurai, more information can be found at www.natori.co.uk

# ABOUT THE AUTHOR

Antony Cummins is the Official Tourism Ambassador for Wakayama, Japan (和歌山市観光発信人) and an author on historical Asian (particularly Japanese) military culture. His intention is to present a historically accurate picture of both samurai and *shinobi* (ninja) to the Western world and lay down the foundations for a better understanding of their teachings and ways. He has published an array of books on Japanese warfare, including translations of historical ninja manuals with his translation partners. Antony and his work can be followed on YouTube under "Samurai and Ninja History", "Natori Ryu" and "Samurai Martial Arts Real Training". For more information see his website: www.natori.co.uk

# ABOUT THE GRAPHIC DESIGNER

Jayson Kane is a Manchester-based graphic designer and illustrator, otherwise known as Kane Kong Illustrates (@kanekongillustrates on Instagram). He studied art, design and print-making, specializing in visual communication. Having worked with Antony Cummins for many years, his portfolio includes: *True Path of the Ninja* (cover concept designer), *The Secret Traditions of the Shinobi* (front cover designer), *Iga and Koka Ninja Skills* (internal illustrations), *The Illustrated Guide to Viking Martial Arts* (internal illustrations), *Ninja Skills* (internal illustrations), *Old Japan* (internal illustrations), *Modern Ninja Warfare* (internal illustrations), *The Ultimate Art of War* (internal illustrations) and *How to Be a Modern Samurai* (internal illustrations).

# ACKNOWLEDGEMENTS

I would like to thank the following people, who have all supported my projects: Alex Hammond, Alexander Farriell, Amamiya, Andrew Dawson, Christopher Lyons, Clarence Sheets, Clayton Tucker, Coach Boavida, Craig Andrew, Jonathan Brook, Kenneth Borr, Matthew Mallozzi, Markus Heil, Mikael Bergstrom, Neil Hurst, Nicholas Mayer, Par Skoglund, Pierre-Alain Chabot, Scholar Studies, Stephen Rosas, Thomas Jenny and Travis Smith.

With special thanks to **Steven Nojiri**, who helped me understand the history, teachings and mechanics of Buddhism in preparation for this book. However, any mistakes made are mine and not his.